# CONTEMPLATIVE ETHICS

## AN INTRODUCTION

Dennis J. Billy, CSsR

PAULIST PRESS
New York/Mahwah, NJ

Cover and book design by Lynn Else

Library of Congress Cataloging-in-Publication Data

Billy, Dennis Joseph.
    Contemplative ethics : an introduction / Dennis J. Billy.
        p. cm.
    Includes bibliographical references.
    ISBN 978-0-8091-4680-2 (alk. paper)
    1. Christian ethics—Catholic authors. I. Title.

BJ1249.B49 2011
241'.042—dc22
                                                        2010038012

Published by Paulist Press
997 Macarthur Boulevard
Mahwah, New Jersey 07430

www.paulistpress.com

Printed and bound in the
United States of America

In fond memory of
my confrere, good friend, and classmate
Pasquale Tremonte, CSsR
(1929–2005)

*"Duc in altum"*
*"Put out into the deep water"*

Luke 5:4

*Duc in altum!* These words ring out for us today, and they invite us to remember the past with gratitude, to live the present with enthusiasm and to look forward to the future with confidence. "Jesus Christ is the same yesterday and today and forever" (Heb 13:8).

Pope John Paul II

# Contents

# Acknowledgments

Earlier versions of material in this book have appeared elsewhere under the following titles:

"What Is Contemplative Ethics?" *Josephinum Journal of Theology* 13 (2006): 2–16 [Chapter One].

"Contemplating the Eternal Word," *Josephinum Journal of Theology* 13 (2006): 209–22 [Chapter Two].

"Contemplating the Incarnate Word," *Josephinum Journal of Theology* 14 (2007): 45–57 [Chapter Three].

"Contemplating the Life and Ministry of Christ: Emerging Guidelines for Christian Living," *Studia moralia* 46 (2008): 433–53 [Chapter Four].

# Introduction

In recent years, Catholic moral theologians have written a number of studies on the connection between their discipline and Christian spirituality.[1] Although these works have provided great insights into the general contours of this relationship, they have not gone very far into particulars.

A few years ago, I took a small step in remedying this situation by looking at the relationship between conscience and prayer in the Catholic spiritual moral tradition.[2] With the same end in mind, I later worked on a second study that focused on the Eucharist and moral living.[3] These collaborative efforts with James Keating were well received and managed to bring a deeper level of theological discourse to the discussion about the relationship between spirituality and moral theology. They have also encouraged me to explore the particulars of this relationship still further.

In the present volume, I intend to probe the relationship between spirituality and moral theology from yet another perspective, this time by looking at the common ground shared by contemplation and the spiritual moral life. I hope to enrich both disciplines by showing how they can relate to one another on equal footing and in a genuine spirit of cooperation. In doing so, I seek to respond to the challenge put forth by the late Pope John Paul II to all the Catholic faithful to "put out into the deep water" ("*Duc in altum*")[4] as they navigate the waters of the new millennium.

Contemplation, for me, is a wordless, thoughtless pondering of an object in childlike wonder. We can contemplate just about anything: ourselves, other people, the world around us, even the divine mysteries. In the latter case, contemplation can be natural (acquired) or infused (mystical), depending on whether God is the primary or secondary agent involved. When I think of contemplation, I often envision a man or woman gazing in wordless silence upon an icon of Christ or the Blessed Mother. He or she does nothing but look upon the sacred representation in the hope of gaining a glimpse into the world beyond. Such a person seeks to commune with God, not on the level of thought, but of spirit. When gazing upon an icon in contemplative prayer, a person allows his or her spirit to cross the threshold of the sacred and commune with God's Holy Spirit. This experience of union comes, not from a person's efforts, but from God as a gift. The person gazing, we might say, is also gazed upon by God, who uses the icon as a window through which the eye of what is infinitely sacred establishes contact with the eye of the soul.

Contemplation is not opposed to thought, but seeks a deeper level of it, the underlying unity beneath the myriad distinctions of rational discourse. It is born of solitude of heart and is sometimes the fruit of meditative prayer, where thoughts, images, and affections are ordered to God in a more quiet, reflective fashion.[6] Although not everyone may be called to the heights of mystical prayer, everyone, I believe, is called to foster a contemplative attitude toward life.[7] I also believe that moral theologians should bring this contemplative attitude into play in the work they do in service to the Church and to the world.

I have consciously selected the challenging and even provocative phrase *contemplative ethics* to describe this intimate relationship between Catholic moral theology and spirituality because of the unsettling (perhaps even disconcerting) effect it will probably have on those who still insist on separating the spiritual and moral spheres of human existence. Although it is a relatively recent phrase in the vocabulary of theological discourse, it represents a venerable and longstanding approach to the spiritual moral life in Catholic thought: one that values contemplation and learning as a true path to wisdom, and that values holiness of life as a means to the experiential knowledge of the divine.[8] It is my belief that Catholic moral theology needs to retrieve this valuable and insightful approach to the spiritual moral life. If Catholic moral theology fails to incorporate a contemplative attitude toward life into its methodology, discourse, and way of thinking, it will in effect be disregarding the millions of believers today who want their reasons for acting to flow from the deep spiritual hungers of their hearts. The true depths of these hungers, I believe, are laid bare in the person of Jesus Christ. By contemplating his face and the mystery of his existence, we hope to gain insights into our own hearts and begin to understand what kinds of actions are both worthy and expected of us.

I have divided the book into six chapters, each of which focuses on a specific element of our study of contemplation and the moral life. In chapter 1, I examine the nature of contemplative ethics and develop a methodology that allows us to explore the anthropological dimensions of contemplative decision making. I then apply this contemplative methodology to the Eternal Word (chapter 2), the Incarnate Word (chapter 3), Jesus' life and ministry (chapter 4), his suffering and death (chapter 5), and his risen life (chapter 6). Near the end of each chapter, I offer a variety of guidelines for the spiritual moral life that flow directly from this contemplative approach to the mysteries of Christ. Some of these guidelines resurface at later moments in the book, in much the same way that deeply rooted attitudes and ways of thinking influence us at not just one but many stages of our lives. As such, they represent recurrent themes or leitmotifs important to our contemplative approach to Catholic moral theology. To engage my readers on a still deeper level, I also offer a series of reflection questions under the title, "Contemplating the Face of

Christ," to help them ponder these mysteries and probe more deeply into their own attitudes about the nature of the spiritual moral life. At the end of each chapter, I also include a practical exercise entitled "Following the Promptings of the Spirit," to provide my readers with some concrete suggestions on how they might deepen their experience of prayer and so live the Gospel on a deeper level of consciousness.[9]

My hope in this book is to point out the close bond between contemplation and action for Christian living and to highlight how immersing ourselves in the mystery of Christ affects the way we think about the nature and scope of our action in the world. I do not claim that my approach is the sole factor to be taken into account when making decisions about the spiritual moral life, only that it has been long overlooked in Catholic moral theological discourse and needs to be retrieved if that discipline is to respond effectively to the mounting challenges of the day. The task for Catholic moral theology today is to foster an ongoing integration of spirituality and morality, contemplation and action, goodness and holiness in the lives of the people it seeks to serve. I hope this book makes a small yet lasting contribution to this important theological undertaking.

# CHAPTER ONE

# What Is Contemplative Ethics?

There is in us a certain root that plunges into the depths of the Trinity. We are these complex beings who exist on successive levels, on an animal and biological level, on an intellectual and human level and on an ultimate level in those very abysses that are those of the life of God and those of the Trinity. This is why we have the right to say that Christianity is an integral humanism, which is to say, which develops man on all levels of his experience. We must always be in defiance of all attempts to reduce the space in which our existence moves. We breathe fully in the measure to which we do not let ourselves be enclosed in the prison of the rational and psychological world but to which a part of us emerges into these great spaces that are those of the Trinity. And this is what creates the incomparable joy of existence in Christianity.

Jean Daniélou, *Myth and Mystery*[1]

To move forward, Catholic moral theology in the twenty-first century must break out of its self-imposed prison of the rational and psychological world that has shaped much of its past and root itself in an integral trinitarian humanism that sincerely seeks to contemplate the face of Christ. If our decisions are to be authentic, we must base them, not merely on the reasoning power of the mind, but also on the tender yet challenging voice of God deep within our hearts. Our decisions must flow from our whole being and give special heed to that dimension of our lives that plunges into the depths of the Trinity. The field of contemplative ethics is an innovative and highly relevant way of doing so. It understands moral decision making in the larger context of humanity's divinization by the trinitarian God and affirms our need to listen attentively to every dimension of our human makeup.

# Contemplation and Ethics

To some, the phrase *contemplative ethics* may seem to involve an inherent contradiction. To contemplate is to speculate in a theoretical and abstract way. It comes from the Greek word *theoria*, which refers to direct and immediate intellectual knowledge.[2] To contemplate can also mean to ponder or meditate upon an object for a certain period of time. When applied to prayer, it involves opening up our heart in faith to the divine and simply resting in it. For Christians at prayer, contemplation *(contemplatio)* means being still in the presence of God. It can be man-made or God-given, that is to say, attained through human effort or through divine intervention. It differs from vocal prayer *(oratio)* and meditation *(meditatio)* in that it quiets both voice and mind in order to commune with God on the deepest level of human existence.[3] It requires an act of the whole person, but in a different way from other types of prayer in that it can lead to direct and immediate experiential knowledge of the divine. "We become contemplatives," Thomas Merton reminds us, "when God discovers Himself in us."[4] Contemplative prayer, in this respect, is mystical prayer. It seeks God in order to repose in God. It asks nothing of God other than to share in the intimacy of the divine friendship. This intimacy comes from God, rises from deep within the human heart, and pours itself out to others in acts of loving service. In this way, the life of contemplation is intimately connected to a life of action.

Ethics, by way of contrast, has to do with a focused application of concrete principles to daily life. It is a practical science having to do with ascertaining the proper course of action to be taken in a given set of circumstances. It discerns what is rational in a given situation and encourages us to act accordingly. According to Aristotle, whose use of the Greek term *ethike* ("ethics") eventually made it a mainstay of Western philosophical discourse, it is the study of human action with regard to the ultimate end of human life. It is also related conceptually to the Greek word *praxis* ("activity"), which, in contrast to contemplation, typically refers to the practical knowledge needed for action in the world.[5] There are a variety of approaches to ethics today, since numerous understandings of man's ultimate end and the nature of human reason have developed over time.[6] Some would maintain a strict separation between what has come to be called "speculative" reason and "practical" reason and would consider a phrase such as contemplative ethics to be nothing but sheer nonsense. Others would allow for various degrees of interaction, depending on the context in which human rationality has been historically and culturally conditioned over time. Still others (like me) would affirm the essential unity of human reason and identify it as a constituent element of human nature.

Depending on our understanding of the nature of human reason, therefore, the phrase *contemplative ethics* may or may not seem a contradiction in terms. Contemplation involves the speculative reason; ethics, the practical. Contemplation ponders the first causes of things; ethics looks for the practical consequences of these causes in everyday life. One involves abstraction and simple presence; the other, the application of principles and concrete practice. Generally speaking, both are related to action, albeit in different ways and for different purposes. While there are many types of contemplation and a variety of different ethics, the two are rarely thought of as operating at the same time and for the same purpose. For many, one has little, if anything, to do with the other. More often than not, they are contrasted or even directly opposed to one another.

I have chosen the phrase *contemplative ethics* not to confuse but to emphasize the important interrelationship between contemplation and action and to highlight the significance of this relationship for the future of Catholic moral theology. I use it as a way of integrating the insights gained from the fruitful discussion on the relationship between spirituality and Catholic moral theology over the past quarter of a century.[7] By this phrase and through the insights that flow from it, I hope to move this discussion forward by proposing a way of spiritual moral decision making that includes not only sound rational reflection, but a process of active listening to every dimension of human existence. When making important decisions, we need to take time to listen to and dialogue with the various aspects of our human makeup, if for no other reason than to be in touch with our genuine needs and come to an adequate understanding of how they can be satisfied. Otherwise, we run the risk of separating the spiritual from the moral spheres of human existence, with the latter devolving into a shallow and empty moralism. Merton puts it this way: "If our prayer is the expression of a deep and grace-inspired desire for newness of life—and not the mere blind attachment to what has always been familiar and 'safe'—God will act in us and through us to renew the Church by preparing, in prayer, what we cannot yet imagine or understand."[8]

In keeping with the above insights, I have divided my presentation into five distinct yet closely related areas. The first treats the various dimensions of contemplation. The second deals with the anthropological aspects of contemplative decision making. The third examines the continuity in relationship between what I call "inward" contemplation and "outward" contemplation. The fourth looks at the spiritual moral consequences of contemplative decision making for the life of the believer. The final section offers relevant remarks on the process of contemplative decision making itself. The goal here is to provide a general description of contemplative ethics and to point out new areas for Catholic moral theology to explore in the twenty-first century.

# The Dimensions of Contemplation

We can begin by saying that there are both inward and outward dimensions to the action of contemplation and that each embraces all levels of our human makeup. The distinction between inward and outward is similar to the discussion in trinitarian theology concerning God's immanent relations and his external actions in the world. The inward action of contemplation corresponds to God's interior gaze upon the Divine Self (that is, upon the immanent trinitarian relations of Father, Son, and Spirit); the outward, to God's external gaze upon his activity in the world (that is, the work of creation, redemption, and sanctification).[9] God, in other words, relates inwardly to himself as Father, Son, and Spirit and also outwardly to the world as Creator, Redeemer, and Sanctifier. The basis for applying this analogy to humanity comes from our being created in the image of God *(imago Dei)*[10] and our ongoing transformation in the life of the Spirit.

When seen in this light, four distinct yet related levels of contemplative activity exist in God and humanity:

1. God's inward contemplation of the Divine Self
2. God's outward contemplation of creation
3. Our participation in God's inward contemplative activity
4. Our subsequent participation of God's outward contemplative activity

God's contemplation, we might say, moves in two directions, and we share in this twofold movement when we ponder ourselves and the world around us. Speculative reason and practical reason are thus closely related, like two sides of the same coin: theory leads to practice, while practice flows from theory. Both represent different modes of a single, ongoing contemplative activity: one that is oriented toward being; the other, toward action.

Another way of looking at these activities would be to examine an ordinary parent-child relationship from everyday life. Take, for example, the loving relationship between a father and his young son. The father has the capacity to reflect on and engage both himself and the world around him. The son, in turn, looks up to his father and desires to be like him in all things. While he has a natural capacity to imitate his father, he is also helped by his father through various pointers and lessons from life. They do things together—fish, play ball, work on the car, take long walks, clean up the yard—and develop over time a close bond of love-affection for one another. The son, we might say, shares in the life of his father, and the father in that of his son. The resulting bond draws them close to each other in a single activity of loving communion.

These dynamics of the parent-child relationship are nothing but a reflection of our capacity to share in God's contemplative activity. What is more, since the tenets of the Christian faith tell us that God is not only Father, but also Son and Spirit, it follows that the loving dynamics of the parent-child relationship lie with the very nature of the Godhead and that our desire to be like God is itself a reflection of the divine.

Theologians have pondered these dynamics for centuries and have concluded that the various levels of contemplative action rest on the supposition of the self-diffusive nature of the good, the transforming (as opposed to merely "enveloping" or "cloaking") nature of grace, and the underlying assertion that we are "capable of receiving God" *(capax Dei)*.[11] If their true natures are to be adequately discerned and appreciated, the inward and outward dimensions of our contemplation of the divine must be viewed within this wider context. Only then can both dimensions be understood as a continuation of the ongoing creative, redemptive, and sanctifying action of the Trinity in the world. Only then can they be seen as a radical expression of the same relations of selfless love existing within the immanent contemplation of the Godhead. Only then will contemplative prayer be understood as being simultaneously oriented toward God and the world; that is, its inward dimension radically oriented toward the outer—and vice versa.

From this perspective, contemplative prayer is an activity of the whole person that rests in and communes with the inward relations and outward expressions of the Trinity itself. To contemplate the presence of God, in other words, means to share in the active and dynamic relations of the Father, Son, and Spirit as they relate to each other and to their creation. This sharing, moreover, takes place on every level of human existence, all of which are required if we truly wish to be still in the presence of God.

# The Human Dimensions of Contemplative Decision Making

The levels in question include the physical, emotional, mental, spiritual, and social elements of human experience.[12] Contemplative decision making is, first of all, an embodied activity. It takes place in the flesh and orients us toward God and world through the body. The physical dimension of human existence cannot be peeled off and discarded at will. Dualisms that denigrate the body or relegate it to an inferior position overlook the nobility of the visible world and the solidarity humanity shares with its physical environs. We are *physical* beings. Our bodies are not some superficial veneer, but an essential dimension of our makeup. The decisions we make have direct consequences for this corporeal dimension of our lives. It is important that we consider these consequences when we make our choices. The Christian doctrine of the resurrection emphasizes the intimate relationship we have to our bodies and to all of creation. When making decisions, we must listen to what the body and the world around us are telling us, identify their aspirations and needs, and respond accordingly.

Contemplative decision making, moreover, is an emotional activity. That is not to say that it is unstable, erratic, or in any way disruptive, but that the activity of resting in God has a calming effect on the emotions and gradually brings them under the gentle sway of reason's benevolent rule. Denying our emotions to ourselves, to others, or to God works against the goal of intimate union with the divine found at the very heart of all contemplative action. We are *emotional* beings. When making decisions, we need to take time to consider our feelings. These too are a constituent element of our human makeup. Rather than ignoring them, giving them mere token recognition, or, worse yet, repressing them (an activity that can only go on for so long), we must allow them time to speak and ourselves time to evaluate them. Only by entering into dialogue with our feelings can we understand what they are telling us about ourselves. Only by identifying them, listening to them, and taking ownership of them can we understand their repercussions for our lives and allow them to inform our decisions.

For this reason, contemplative decision making is also a mental activity. It does not relish ideas for their own sake and is very conscious of their limitations as vehicles leading to the experience of the divine. It recognizes, however, the importance of relating to God with a quiet mind and is conscious of the great difficulty with which it is achieved. Contemplation does not deny the importance of ideas; it merely puts them in perspective. It requires the intelligence to understand that human experience is multidimensional and that intellectual pursuits, however noble, do not exhaust the depths of the human heart. We are *intellectual* beings. We have the gift of self-consciousness and are able to reflect upon our experience and learn from our past. What is more, we are able to analyze the various factors involved in a decision and view them from a variety of perspectives. We have the use of reason and are able to use it for good or for ill. Through our use of reason, we are able to communicate both with ourselves and with one another. Because we are rational beings, we are able to create thoughts and concepts that help to shape our physical and cultural environments. For these reasons, it is important that, when making decisions, we have a clear idea of what specifically "is on our mind." Only by allowing our thoughts to unfold will we be able to appraise them and eventually identify those worth pursuing.

And only then can contemplation be understood as a spiritual activity. In many ways, this is the deepest dimension of human existence; that is, where the human spirit opens up to, rests in, and communes with the divine. When the human spirit communes with God in this way, the resulting experience of intimacy overflows, be it ever so slightly, into every other anthropological dimension and effects our gradual transformation. This overflow necessarily affects our relationships with others and the world they live in. We are *spiritual* beings. We yearn for self-transcendence and look for ways to unite ourselves with what brings us into being and sustains us there from one moment to the next. The spiritual dimension of our makeup reflects our deepest longings. It touches human consciousness, but lies largely beneath the level of rational reflection in the area of the subconscious. When making decisions, we need to allow our spirits to rise to the surface of our awareness and find expression. To do so, we need to put aside our thoughts, to quiet our minds, and to soak in the silence around us. Only by giving our spirits the opportunity to breathe in the surrounding stillness will we

allow that side of our human makeup to participate in our decisions. The human spirit speaks not through words and concepts,
but through an intuitive sense. We will never be in touch with
that sense if we do not give the deepest dimension of our lives the
opportunity and time to express itself.

For this reason, contemplative decision making is also considered a preeminently social activity. The trinitarian God is relational by its very nature; to contemplate God thus involves an
intrinsically communal activity. Even when we contemplate
God in private, we are opening up to the social dimension of the
divine and, by virtue of the mystery of the incarnation, we are
tied to the rest of humanity by a bond of solidarity through
Christ's Body, the Church. We are *social* beings. We exist, not as
isolated individuals, but as members of the human family. We
develop physically, emotionally, intellectually, and spiritually
only as members of a community, one that exists on many levels
(for example, family, church, town, nation, and so forth). When
we make decisions, it is important that we take these various levels of our human family into account. Our actions have consequences, not just for us as individuals, but for the various groups
to which we belong. When we make decisions, it is important
that we talk them over with representatives of those groups most
affected by the consequences of our actions. We should also be
willing to assist others in their attempts to reach a prudential
course of action for their lives. We are who we are by virtue of
our membership in human society. Our decisions should reflect
responsible membership in that society.

All of these dimensions are important elements of contemplative decision making. To omit any one of them would be to
denigrate the act of contemplation itself and ultimately deny an
essential element of humanity's makeup. For contemplative
decision making to take place, all of these dimensions must be
acknowledged and thoroughly integrated in our lives. That does
not mean, however, that they will exist in the same proportions

in each individual. There are probably as many different ways of contemplating God as there are individual human beings. In contemplative decision making, each of us will emphasize these elements in slightly different ways, thus making the action uniquely our own.

To help us along, it is also important to remember that the Holy Spirit moves us on every level of our human makeup through gifts and inspired promptings. It does so by acting through our emotions and the rational powers of our souls to affect every dimension of our existence, either directly or indirectly, to help us become fully ourselves before God and humanity. The Spirit, we might say, graces us with its gifts and empowers us to share both in God's inner life and in his outward expression of love for all creation. It is through the Spirit that we experience and understand what it means to love; it is through the Spirit that we share in God's creative, redemptive, and sanctifying mission.

To return to the father-son analogy, the Spirit is like the strong, loving bond that a son shares with his father and that guides him even when away from his father. This bond is even stronger than death and helps the son long after his father is gone—and vice versa. The strength of the father-son relationship is powerfully presented in Jesus' parable of the Prodigal Son (also known as the parable of the Merciful Father). The parable reminds us of the unconditional nature of love and its power to heal and forgive even under the most difficult of circumstances.[13]

# The Inward and Outward Dimensions of Contemplation

As might be expected, these various factors function differently in the inward and outward actions of contemplation. While inward contemplation is concerned with the process of becoming still before God, outward contemplation seeks to carry that stillness into everyday life. The former focuses on the discipline of quieting ourselves before God on every level of our lives, while the latter concerns itself with actively bringing the rest of life in accord with that experience. Concretely speaking, inward contemplation seeks the stillness of embodied place, the serenity of a calm emotional life, the restful gaze of the intellect, the transcendent longing of the spirit, and harmonious relations with others. Outward contemplation is continuous with all of these, but seeks to bring the contemplating activity to where it is in need of strengthening or has never been before. As such, it has a very difficult task to perform, for it must seek to maintain the sense of stillness in the presence of God in the midst of a world of action. It seeks embodied quiet, emotional stillness, intellectual rest, spiritual peace, and communal harmony—all in the midst of vigorous action.

The aspect of activity in the world distinguishes outward from inward contemplation and represents its culminating function. Inward contemplation, in other words, is intrinsically oriented toward the outward—and vice versa. This circular relationship means that outward contemplation is already implicitly present in the act of inward contemplation itself and that inward contemplation is both the source and goal toward which outward contemplation tends. When seen in this light, the various dimensions of inward and outward contemplation enjoy this same reciprocal relationship. That is to say that the physical-emotional-mental-spiritual-social dimensions of inward contemplation are intrinsically oriented toward outward activity. Once "in action," they remain both the source and goal toward which the anthropological dimensions of outward contemplation tend. From this perspective, the inward/outward nomenclature can be further divided into two other recognizable contemplative activities that would require the participation of all the various anthropological dimensions outlined above. A fourfold continuum thus arises: inward contemplation—inward contemplation looking outward—outward contemplation looking inward—outward contemplation. The first of the middle two terms describes inward contemplation as it moves toward a self-diffusive expression in the outward; the second describes outward contemplation with a strong inward dimension to it.

This way of presenting the relationship between inward and outward contemplation has a number of distinct advantages. For one thing, it avoids the misleading impression that the two activities of contemplation exist in a disjunctive relationship or can in any way be dichotomized. For another, it accurately conveys the sense in which outward contemplation already begins in the act of inward contemplation and then actively carries it over into a life of action in the world. The variety of moments along the continuum also provides a helpful context for understanding the relation between contemplation and action. The relationship of reciprocity highlights the intimate connection between inward and outward contemplation, without compromising their clearly discernible differences. By drawing tighter bonds between "contemplation of being" and "contemplation in action," the continuum also provides deeper insights into the deep influence contemplation can have on the transformation of human society and the world beyond.

To return once again to the father-son analogy, we can explain the various dimensions of contemplation in this way: To begin with, the father and son may choose to simply rest in their intimate bond of love (inward contemplation). In time, they may ponder what it may be like to express this love outwardly to others (inward contemplation looking outward). When they finally decide to express this love to others, they will often look back to the bond that sustains them and keeps them close (outward contemplation looking inward). Eventually, they come to see that their bond is so strong that they carry it with them in all that they do (outward contemplation). These various dimensions of contemplative activity build upon one another and are oriented toward the outward expression of loving service.

## Spiritual Moral Dimensions

The spiritual moral implications of this fourfold continuum are closely aligned with the anthropological factors discussed earlier. Each moment in the continuum displays an array of ethical considerations involving the whole person.

### LOOKING INWARD

This moment of human contemplative activity is concerned with stillness in the presence of God. It focuses its attention away from outward interaction with the world and toward the contemplation of the divine realities. Depending on whether it is acquired or infused, this simple contemplative activity is predominantly either a human or divine action. It is fundamentally relational in nature and has an important transformative effect on us. By orienting us entirely to the contemplation of the divine, we place before God whatever anthropological dissonance we may be experiencing. Opening up our lives to God in this way relativizes that dissonance and helps us to look forward to the day of its passing. Inward contemplation thus gives rise to an ever-deepening experience of Christian hope.

As an embodied action, it affirms the goodness of the physical world and the importance of caring for our health and bodily well-being. As an affective action, it rejoices in the full potential of the emotions, which can be cultivated only when they are trained by reason's gentle rule to avoid the extremes of excess and defect. As a mental activity, it reaffirms God as the teleological point of all human endeavor and the means by which we reach our final end. As a spiritual activity, it communes with God's Spirit and yearns for the day when the fullness of union with God will end its restless longings. As a social activity, it recognizes its bonds of solidarity with all people by virtue of their common human dignity (as *imago Dei*) and their incorporation in Christ's Body, the Church. The inward contemplation of God helps us to keep alive the hope for the radical anthropological transformation of ourselves—and of all humanity. These particular and universal dimensions of inward contemplation pour out onto the other moments of the continuum and manifest themselves in very particularized moral categories.

## LOOKING OUTWARD FROM WITHIN

This moment of human contemplative activity remains essentially inward, but has partially shifted its gaze from God to human society and the world around it. The shift is only partial because this moment presupposes and remains continuous with what went before it. It is not a question of inward contemplation simply ceasing and giving way to one that is more concerned with the world around it. Rather, it is about our becoming so caught up in an intimate relationship with God (that is, inward contemplation) that we are led to ponder what might be done to alleviate the world from its afflictions (that is, inward contemplation looking outward). The latter contemplative activity has a transformative effect on the various dimensions of human existence, thus making it qualitatively different from simply "thinking about what can be done to improve the world." It is not a retreat from God, but a participatory journey into the Trinity's ongoing activity in the world.

Contemplating the world in this way is an embodied activity that establishes deeper bonds between the world within and the world without. It seeks to overcome the limitations of the traditional subject/object distinction and to help those contemplating to see the deep bonds connecting him or her to the surrounding environment. Contemplating the world in this way makes us examine any emotional responses to particular situations that might veer off into exaggerated, irrational extremes. At the same time, it requires us to examine our heart and to discern which just causes we might be willing (and able) to adopt. Contemplating the world in this way asks us to take a critical look at the world and society in which we live. It means being willing to penetrate appearances, to discover the root causes of hatred and injustice, and to search for reasonable solutions in accord with Gospel values. Contemplating the world in this way requires us to discern the spirits at work in the world and to find ways of cooperating with those working for humanity's good. Contemplating the world in this way helps us to see all of humanity in the individual and the individual in all of humanity. It deepens our respect for human existence and encourages us to move the process of contemplation to fruitful outward action.

## LOOKING INWARD FROM WITHOUT

This moment of contemplative activity remains essentially outward, but still maintains a very strong and visibly discernible inward dimension. Here, those contemplating have taken very concrete steps to have an impact on the surrounding world, yet need long periods of quiet inward contemplative activity to sustain those efforts. Like the previous moment of contemplative activity, this moment is a mixture of the inward and outward dimensions of contemplation. It differs from the previous one, however, in that its focus is more visibly rooted in activity in the world. This moment of contemplative activity is in continuity with the previous one and actually presupposes it. It would be impossible to initiate and sustain prolonged contemplative action in the world without having first taken the time to ponder the situation at depth and to let it unfold in our heart in the presence of God. To do so would disrupt the continuum of contemplative activity outlined above and to turn our action in the world into a mere rational reflection on the practical order. This moment should be understood as an extension of, and, in fact, even a deepening of, the previous one. As those contemplating become more and more immersed in action in the outward order, they will find less and less of a need for explicitly inward contemplation. The reason for this is not because inward contemplation is no longer necessary, but because it has gradually been subsumed into the outward activity itself.

Acting in the world in this way helps us to foster a contemplative attitude toward life. It enables us to view the environment not as something to be manipulated for our own benefit, but as something to be cared for and nurtured with gratitude and respect. Acting in the world in this way helps us, not to "act out" of our emotions, but to integrate them in a reflective manner so that they will help to further our goals for a just and lasting peace. Acting in the world in this way enables us to reflect upon and then to prioritize our needs in such a way that God and God's creation rather than the self and self-creation are at the center of our worldview. Acting in the world in this way helps us to see beneath the appearances of things and to attribute a central role to the anthropological dimension of spirit in the unfolding of human action. Acting in the world in this way affirms our commitment to human solidarity, for it demonstrates by means of concrete outward activity that we have truly assimilated the human universal as an object of contemplation and made it our own.

## LOOKING OUTWARD

This final moment of contemplative activity represents a merging of contemplative categories. By this time, the assimilation of inward contemplation by outward contemplation taking place during the previous moment has reached its climax. Now inward contemplation and outward contemplation are completely one. The subject/object dichotomy has completely broken down. Action in the world is no longer considered apart from our inward contemplation and search for God. The two have now become so intimately tied that they can no longer be distinguished. This means that we contemplate God in and through our activity in the world and that we act in the world when contemplating God. This moment represents the fullness of contemplative activity—and also the beginning. It does not get us lost in activity for activity's sake, but carries our actions to the threshold of the sacred. There, we wish only to sit in the stillness of God's presence so that we can listen and respond with God to the exigencies of the present moment. Time itself takes on a different texture: *chronos* gradually gives way to *kairos*; we find that we are more and more able to celebrate the sacrament of the present moment.[14]

Acting in the world in this way is the fullness of contemplation. It celebrates the embodiment of time and space in the divine embrace and recognizes humanity's contemplative action in the world as an instrument of God's transforming presence. Acting in the world in this way helps us to discern in the world and in human society the vestiges of the divine affections that brought them forth and that continue to hold them in being. It sees the world as an expression of God's deep and effusive desire to love and to be loved. Acting in the world in this way helps us to become more aware of the Wisdom of God in the book of creation and in the book of life. It helps us to discern God's hidden but abiding presence in the world and in the human heart. Acting in the world in this way enables us to ponder and to be pondered by the Spirit of God as it broods over the world and acts upon it. It affirms the Spirit as the primary mover in the affairs of the world and the need that all have to exist in harmony with it. Acting in the world in this way acknowledges the close relationship between human contemplation and the activity of the Godhead. In doing so, it enables us to see more clearly the participatory role that all of humanity is called to play in the ongoing creation, redemption, and sanctification of the world.

If we use our imagination, we can see each of these contemplative moments at work in the character of the father in Jesus' parable of the Prodigal Son. The father loves each of his sons and rejoices in their presence in his life from the very first moment they entered his life (looking inward). As they grow from childhood to young adulthood, he ponders their strengths and weaknesses and, like any loving father, wonders what the future might hold for them (looking outward from within). When his younger son leaves home and the older son decides to remain and work the farm, he looks back with nostalgia for what once was and wishes, at least in the case of his younger son, that things had turned out differently (looking inward from without). Finally, when the younger son returns, the father's deep love for his sons moves him to action: he kills the fatted calf and throws a feast for his lost son, and assures his elder son that everything he has is his (looking outward). These contemplative moments mark the depth of the father's love and compassion for his sons. In some way these moments are present in all authentic relationships, most especially in our relationship with God.

# Relevance for Contemplative Ethics

A number of considerations about the process involved in contemplative decision making now come to the fore. Rather than being exhaustive, the remarks that follow seek only to complement what has already been said and possibly identify areas of future development in the field. It goes without saying that each of these attributes is important for any relationship that wishes to reach full maturity.

*Contemplative ethics requires a continuous backdrop of inner silence or solitude of heart.* This backdrop allows us to stay in touch with the various dimensions of our human makeup and permits them to enter fully into our efforts of discernment and moral decision making. This backdrop of inner silence opens our hearts to God, puts us in touch with inner yearnings, and helps us to reflect contemplatively on the practical issues at hand. It does so, not by confusing the contemplative and practical spheres of life, but by allowing them to assist each other by operating simultaneously, yet on different planes.

*Contemplative ethics bids us to consider every dimension of our human makeup in the light of Jesus Christ.* He is the New Man, the one who represents the goal toward which our humanity tends and the person in whom our humanity promises one day to be transformed. Contemplative ethics asks us to recognize the limitations of our broken humanity and to live in hope of the transforming power of Jesus' love for us. We accomplish this by contemplating Christ's humanity and seeing in it a reflection of our own. Jesus has manifested to us the inner life of the trinitarian God and made it accessible to us. Because of his incarnation, passion, death, and resurrection, his face is now our face; his story, our story. Only by contemplating Christ will we ever be able to commune with him and share in his mission.

*Contemplative ethics embraces a threefold movement of contemplation, communion, and mission.* The first effects the second, culminates in the third, and comes back full circle. This circular process holds true both for the life of the Trinity and our own. We give glory to God by participating in the inner and outer life of trinitarian contemplation, communion, and mission.[15] We do so because of Jesus, the Word made flesh, who came to earth specifically to open for us the way to the Father and to offer us life in the Spirit. This life helps us to implement on the human sphere (that is, in our personal lives and social relationships) a reflection of what is already taking place on the level of the divine.

*Contemplative ethics focuses not only on the human actions and virtues needed to perform them, but also on the attitudes we must have to sustain the options we have chosen to direct us.*

These options focus on the underlying interpretations we embrace about the nature of God, the human person, and the world we live in. For Christians, they focus on following Christ and deciding to be a disciple. Attitudes are to options what virtues are to actions. The option to follow Christ precedes the Christian's call to virtuous action. Contemplative ethics brings the option to follow Christ to the forefront of all decision making. Each step of the disciple's journey must be focused on the reason for taking it and the destination he or she has in sight.[16]

*Contemplative ethics encourages serious reflection on particular issues and the decisions to be made concerning them.* It is important to ponder each question from as many angles as possible, always taking into account the teaching of the Church and the specific principles relevant to the topic. In examining the array of options before us, we should carefully weigh the pros and cons of each possibility. Only by analyzing and evaluating a moral concern in an unhurried, reflective manner will we be in a position to decide upon the best course of action to take.

*Contemplative ethics involves naming and taking ownership of our feelings on areas of moral concern.* We should try, not only to identify the range of feelings about particular issues, but also to understand why we feel the way we do about them. By allowing our feelings to surface, we allow another dimension of our human makeup to participate in the decision-making process. As we do so, we should also ask ourselves if our feelings on the matter are appropriate or off the mark. We must be careful not to allow inappropriate feelings to take control of the decision-making process. More often than not, this happens when we ignore or repress our feelings instead of airing them and trying to understand them.

*Contemplative ethics requires identifying the personal and social needs involved in our decisions.* We should be very specific about these needs and as thorough as possible in our assessment of them. Why must we make this decision? How urgent is it? What will each possible choice accomplish? Whom will it benefit? Will the decision meet our most basic needs, satisfy superficial needs, or possibly even create new needs? It often helps to draw up a prioritized list of our needs and relate them to the decision before us. Further questions might then arise about any prior decisions we need to make before dealing with the issue at hand.

*Finally, contemplative ethics bids us to look to the area of concrete action.* We must ask ourselves if we are ready to make a decision. Is the matter as urgent as it first seemed? Do we need more time for reflection? Have we examined every aspect of our human makeup? Have we done so in the light of our faith in Christ? Is there something else we need to examine? Is there someone with whom we need to talk? We should try to be as realistic and specific as possible about the matter before us. If we sense that we have reached a moment of decision, then we should make it and resolve to implement it in an appropriate and reasonable way. If not, then we should resolve to postpone the decision and resume the process later.

Although many more things can be said about the nature and scope of contemplative ethics, those listed above make considerable headway into identifying its primary characteristics and the process involved in implementing it. If nothing else, they point out areas of concern for involving the whole person in the process of moral decision making.

# Conclusion

What is contemplative ethics? It is a process of seemingly contrary interactions: contemplation in action and action in contemplation. It insists that human contemplation must be viewed in the larger context of divine contemplation, which itself can be further reduced to the immanent and external action of the Trinity. Such a context gives human contemplation a participation in the interior and exterior activities of the divine and imparts to it a corresponding structural resemblance. This reflection of the divine in human existence gives the action of contemplation both inward and outward foci, which, upon further analysis, can be further broken down into a fourfold continuum. Each contemplative moment along this continuum embraces every dimension of human existence and has very concrete moral ramifications.

In contemplative ethics, this continuum is circular rather than linear. Each moment presupposes and builds upon the previous one, while the last leads us to contemplating the first. This reciprocal motion reflects a similar relationship of reciprocity within the Trinity itself and its creative, redemptive, and sanctifying action in the world. In this way, each and every moment of human contemplation, wherever it lies along the fourfold continuum, can be considered an analogical extension of the immanent and external actions of the Trinity in the world. As such, each moment can be considered a vestige of the Triune God implanted in human existence and, by further extension, in humanity's action in the world.

In the final analysis, contemplative ethics maintains that God's contemplation of humanity initiates a process of divinization, which manifests itself in our capacity to contemplate God. The selfless nature of God eventually redirects our contemplation of God outward onto ourselves and the world around us. This act of contemplation eventually manifests itself in an act of "contemplation in action," which seeks to transform the world by bringing it in accord with God's providential design. "In order to know and love God as He is," as Merton reminds us, "we must have God dwelling in us in a new and special way."[17] When seen in this light, human contemplation is a creative and dynamic instrument of the divine plan. We can contemplate God only because God is continually contemplating us. The transformation of the world is a cosmological corollary of this one basic insight. Through it, we share in the intimacy of the divine relations and participate in their ongoing missions to the new creation.

## CONTEMPLATING THE FACE OF CHRIST

1. What is your understanding of the relationship between contemplation and ethics? Are they completely separate actions? Are they only loosely related? Are they meant to work in harmony? Do you believe there can be such a thing as a "contemplative ethics"?
2. Do you agree with the general idea of there being different "moments" of contemplation? If so, do you agree with the way they have been presented in this chapter? If not, why not? What would you put in its place? Would you present the moments of contemplation any differently?
3. How is contemplation rooted in the human person? Does it involve all the dimensions of human existence or only a limited number of them? Are there any dimensions of human existence that have been left out of the presentation? If so, how does contemplation relate to them?
4. Do you agree that these various moments have significance for the spiritual moral life? If so, how would you describe this significance? Is there anything you would add to or subtract from the various guidelines listed at the end of the chapter?

## FOLLOWING THE PROMPTINGS OF THE SPIRIT

Read the parable of the Prodigal Son (Luke 15:11–32) in a slow, meditative fashion. After doing so, spend some time in quiet prayer and then reflect upon someone you really care about, but have experienced some tension with in your life: one of your par-

WHAT IS CONTEMPLATIVE ETHICS?

ents or grandparents, a brother or a sister, a close friend, a class-mate, a passing acquaintance. Ponder that person's life, his or her daily activities, strengths and weaknesses, likes and dislikes, the way he or she interacts with you. Try to put yourself in this person's shoes. Contemplate what it would be like to be him or her. Rest a while in silent reflection. After a few minutes, ask yourself some questions: What do you share in common with this person? How do the two of you differ? Does pondering the person in this way make you feel closer to him or her? Does it make you want to act differently toward him or her? If so, how?

# CHAPTER TWO

# Contemplating the Eternal Word

> Because the uniqueness of Christ—his childhood, youth, and manhood; his death, resurrection, and ascension—is from the beginning divine and, hence, beyond time, eternal, no man can outgrow him, but must always go back again from the end to the beginning, in order to find the Alpha again in the Omega, the Omega already present in the Alpha, together with all the intermediate stages. A Christian has to learn to see the suffering Christ and the glorified Christ already in the child, the eternal child. Made a child ever anew, he must grow into eternal childhood. It is the same with the adult Christ, suffering and glorified.
>
> Hans Urs von Balthasar[1]

If we are to find the end in the beginning, the last in the first, the Omega already present in the Alpha, then contemplating the face of Christ requires us at some point to ponder the mysterious features of the Eternal Word. This mystery lies beyond our powers of comprehension. We know it only through the loving revelation of the Father, who speaks his Word to us in and through the person of Jesus. In Jesus, the Son of God, the Word receives a concrete, visible countenance. That face ponders us and invites us to behold and contemplate it so that its piercing eyes might look into our own, probe our troubled hearts and consciences, and reveal to us the deepest and most profound mysteries of the Eternal Word.

Those mysteries tell us that the suffering and glorified Christ exists in the very heart of God, even before the historical circumstances of the Christ event. They remind us that the Christ child is also an Eternal Child and that his stages of growth, life, suffering, death, and rebirth reveal as much about the nature of God as they do our own human destiny.[2] They teach us that the life, death, and resurrection of Christ reveal something of the inner life of God and of how we should lead our own lives.

In this chapter, we will explore the spiritual moral significance and consequences of our efforts to contemplate the Eternal Word. In doing so, we will see that Catholic moral theology has its roots in the community of divine love, the strength and power of which helps us to see our own lives together in a different light.

# The Community of Divine Love

The Eternal Word is not a vague and elusive abstraction, but the Wisdom of God, a dynamic presence in the one ultimate reality of Father, Son, and Spirit. It is faceless only from the point of view of human understanding. Were it not for the mystery of the Word made flesh in Jesus of Nazareth, it would have remained forever shrouded in mystery, something beyond our capacity to comprehend. Prior to the incarnation, knowledge of the Word was almost the exclusive domain of esoteric philosophical speculation and Greek translations of concepts from the Hebrew Scriptures pertaining to Divine Wisdom.[3] However, after the appearance of the Risen Lord and the sending of the Holy Spirit at Pentecost, the Christian community's ongoing reflection on the meaning of the Christ event gave rise to the profound realization that the Eternal Word had entered the realm of human existence in the person of Jesus of Nazareth. This recognition led to the development of the doctrine of the Trinity, a teaching that lies at the top of the Church's doctrinal hierarchy of truths and to which all subsequent teaching (including those regarding morals) must ultimately refer.

Succinctly stated in the Creed that we recite at Mass on Sundays and solemn feasts, the doctrine of the Trinity affirms the existence of three Divine Persons in one God. The first is the almighty Father, "maker of heaven and earth, and of all that is, seen and unseen." The second is the one Lord, Jesus Christ, who, as the only Son of God, is eternally begotten of the Father: "God from God, Light from Light, true God from true God." The third is the Holy Spirit, "the Lord and giver of life, who proceeds from the Father and the Son, who with the Father and Son is worshipped and glorified."[4] This creedal affirmation of a Trinity— three Persons in one God: Father, Son, and Spirit: all consubstantial yet relationally distinct—reveals something very important about the nature of the internal life within the Godhead.

One of the greatest contributions of the doctrine of the Trinity to the history of ideas is that it places the concept of "relation" within the very nature of God.[5] The ungenerated Father, the generated Son, and the processing Spirit are distinct from one another by virtue of their differences in relationship, making the Godhead relational in its very essence. But since Essence and Being are identical in God, the contrary conclusion must also be true: the Divinity is distinct by virtue of its oneness in Being, and one by virtue of its distinctive relationships. The relations that differentiate the Persons are united by virtue of the latter's oneness in Being; the oneness in Being that unites the Persons is itself differentiated by virtue of the latter's relations. Unity and multiplicity, therefore, find their resolution in the metaphysical juxtaposition of Being and Relation in the mystery of God's eternal Love. Such is the incomprehensible mystery of the relational God of the Christian faith, expressed so eloquently in the tradition by the simple term *Trinitas.*[6]

# The Eternal Word

A genuine Christian reflection on the Eternal Word must take into account the mysteries of both the Trinity *and* the incarnation. We must not confuse the distinctive priorities of each of these mysteries to the Word. The first has a metaphysical priority in that the Word has existed from all eternity in a loving communal relationship with the Father and the Spirit. The second has an epistemological priority in that we have come to know of its existence (and the Trinity's as well) only through the Church's reflection on the revelation of the Word made flesh in the person of Jesus Christ. Each of these relationships—to the Trinity and to the incarnation—tells us much about the nature of the Eternal Word and its relevance for our lives.

## LOGOS AND TRINITY

When we ponder the mystery of the Trinity, the Word presents itself to us as the Divine Logos, the perfect expression of the Father. This utterance is not merely a personal articulation of the divine, but an actually existing Person, who shares its Being with the Father and relates to him as his only begotten Son.[7] As the eternally generated Son, the Word shares with the Father a deep bond of love: The Father speaks; the Son humbly listens. The Son selflessly reflects back to the Father; the Father welcomes this action of selfless offering and returns his love accordingly. From this intimate and eternal action of giving and receiving proceeds the Holy Spirit, the bond of love between the Father and the Son, who also is an existing Person, one in Being with the other Persons of the Trinity.

When contemplating the Word from a trinitarian standpoint, we affirm its relational existence, its receptivity to the Father, its action of selfless offering, and its ongoing communion with the Father and the Spirit. Each of these traits offers a significant contribution to Catholic moral theology as it seeks to integrate a contemplative outlook on life with the important spiritual moral concerns of the day.

## LOGOS AND THE INCARNATION

The relationship between the human and divine in Jesus of Nazareth brings out an altogether different set of traits from those discovered in the Word's relationship to the Trinity. The christological doctrine of the hypostatic union of the divine and human natures in one Divine Person places the Word at the very center of Jesus' earthly sojourn. The Word of God, we are told, is the unique subject of Jesus' birth, growth, public ministry, passion, death, resurrection, and ascension into heaven.[8] Because it is eternal, however, the Word can be the subject of these historical events and transformative processes only if it somehow holds them within itself from all eternity. All things spring from the Wisdom of the Father. As the perfect expression of the Father, the maker of heaven and earth, the Eternal Word contains within it all heavenly and earthly possibilities.

The Christ event is a revelation to humanity precisely because it springs from the Wisdom of the Father. The various details and intricacies of this event have already been conceived in the mysterious depths of the Father's love for humanity. The incarnation represents the beginning implementation of this grand design to effect humanity's redemption, a plan that has its origins in the generous response of divine compassion to humanity's universal sinful shortcomings.

When seen in this light, the mysteries of the Trinity and the incarnation provide the theological and anthropological backdrops against which we contemplate the Eternal Word in relation to God and humanity. Andrei Rublev's sixteenth-century icon *The Holy Trinity* aptly portrays this intimate community of love in which we are called to share. Three visitors in angelic dress gather around a table to partake in a sacred meal. As they sit around the holy table where the meal is being served, their figures form the shape of a chalice, while the dish on the altar contains the sacrifi-  cial lamb, a symbol of the eucharistic Body and Blood of Christ of the new covenant. The circle is completed only by the onlooker, whose faithful gaze upon the icon enables him or her to partake in the sacred meal made possible by God becoming man. The themes indicated by the icon touch upon some of the most fundamental truths of the Christian faith. An icon such as *The Holy Trinity* is meant to help a person experience the doctrines it embodies on a deeply spiritual level. By gazing in silence upon this sacred image, the onlooker enters a window to the sacred, encounters these mysteries on a deeply personal level, and appreciates their implications for everyday life.[9]

# Contemplating the Eternal Word

Rublev's icon enables the mysteries of the Trinity and the incarnation to penetrate the conscious and unconscious dimensions of our lives in the very act of contemplation itself. It reminds us of the intimate connection between theology and spirituality, between faith in search of understanding and life in the Spirit. As Thomas Merton reminds us, "The understanding of dogma is the proximate and ordinary way to contemplation."[10] The Church's teaching, we might say, not only conveys the truths of the faith, but also acts as a medium through which we can experience and live out our lives in relation to God. Keeping in mind this close bond between theology and contemplation, we now turn our attention to what contemplating the Eternal Word can reveal to us about the content and shape of Catholic moral theology.

## LOOKING INWARD

The first moment of human contemplative activity involves stillness in the presence of the Word. God is everywhere. He created the world (and sustains it) through the power of his Eternal Word. This Word mediates the world and all within it to the Father in the Spirit. The Word stands not apart from the world, but within it, in such a way that it allows the world to participate in its existence. The world exists because the Word exists. This participated Being means that there exist vestiges of God in creation. Man, created in the image and likeness of God, is one such vestige, the example par excellence of the impression the Divinity has left of itself in creation. We find ourselves in the presence of the Word when we stand in awe before the beauty of creation and in wonder at our own existence. Humanity represents God's creation becoming conscious of itself. As such, it mirrors the primary function of the Word as the eternal consciousness of the Father.

Our internal contemplation of the Word is not direct, but mediated. We approach it through our contemplation of the world around us and of our own consciousness. Our awareness of our consciousness offers us a faint reflection of the Word as the consciousness of God. We gain a glimpse of the stillness of the Word in the presence of the Father when we allow our own consciousness to be still before the unnamed source from which it comes. Although the distance between our experience of consciousness and that of the Word remains infinitely large, it nonetheless provides us with a faint ray of light with which to approach the ground of our existence and the source from which all things come.

In contemplating that faint ray of light within us and in the world around us, we travel beyond the sphere of consciousness to an intuited experience of primordial Being. We find ourselves in a receptive stance before ultimate reality. Immersed in the dynamic interplay of Being and Becoming from which all things come, we feel embraced (virtually enveloped) by an existence in which we share, but which is also far greater than we are. The Good, we are told, is self-diffusive, for it refuses to contain itself.[11] Our contemplation of the Word as it exists internally within the Godhead puts us in touch with the Son's love for the Father and the Father's love for the Son, which it so perfectly and humbly reflects. That love, the bond of the Spirit that unites them, does not wish to be restrained. It freely pours out its love in the processes of creation, redemption, and sanctification, divine actions that reveal as much about the inner life of God as they do of our human frailty and need for grace.

## LOOKING OUTWARD FROM WITHIN

The second moment of contemplative activity involves gazing upon the Word in its orientation toward the mystery of the incarnation. Although God's Word became flesh at a particular moment in time, its intention to do so existed within the Word from all eternity. The wood of the manger, we might say, existed in God before the star appeared at Bethlehem. At this level of contemplation, our gaze turns away from the Word's place in the Trinity to its specific role in God's plan of salvation. As we ponder the Word in this particular role, we focus on the divine plan prior to its implementation; that is to say, we are pondering, not the Incarnate Word itself, but the orientation of the preexistent Logos toward humanity that would one day culminate in the birth of Jesus.

From all eternity, God's plan was not merely to create the world and sustain its existence moment by moment, nor was it merely to leave traces or vestiges of his presence both there and in the heart of the human person, whom he created in his image and likeness.[12] God's bold intention was to enter his creation and to experience it from the inside looking out. To be authentic, such an experience could not simply be imagined or be the object of mere speculation in the mind of God: it actually had to occur. To experience creation through creation's eyes, God needed to enter into a unique relationship with creation, a union that would be an exception to the rules of the created world and so comprehensive that it would not bear repeating.

It is entirely fitting that the Eternal Word should enter the world through the creature most closely resembling it. Divine consciousness would enter the world through human consciousness by means of an intimate (hypostatic) union of natures, a relationship so unique that it tests the limits of human understanding. With the Word becoming flesh, God would experience creation in an entirely different way. He would relate to it not merely as its creator, but now as its companion and fellow traveler. What is more, the arrival of human freedom and the likelihood of humanity's fall from grace would provide God with yet another reason for entering the finite boundaries of time and space. Humanity's fall came as no surprise to God. He always knew that the sin of human origins would require a unique and original plan to make things right. That plan was not contingent on humanity's fall, but existed firmly in God's mind from all eternity.

In addition to experiencing creation from within, the entrance of the Word into the world would also heal humanity of its self-inflicted wounds and lift it to a higher plane. These two purposes—experiencing creation from within and effecting humanity's redemption—are closely related, since both concern the transformation of the world and humanity's divinization.[13] By entering the world, the Eternal Word would establish a new relationship between itself and creation. By experiencing creation from within, it would unleash a process of transformation that would ultimately lead to a new humanity and a new creation.

Both are the fulfillment of the first creation and existed in the Word from all eternity. Even if there had never been a fall from grace, humanity's divinization and the world's transformation would most assuredly have taken place. When we ponder the Word in this contemplative moment, we stand in awe of the beauty and magnitude of God's providential plan. The mind of God foresees all contingencies and seeks to make all things work for the good.

## LOOKING INWARD FROM WITHOUT

The third moment of human contemplative activity ponders the mystery of the Incarnate Word in its relationship with the Father and the Spirit. When the Word enters our world and unites with human nature, its relationship with the other Persons of the Trinity is neither ended nor obscured. The Word's place within the Trinity remains constant, even as it empties itself to be born in the likeness of man. The self-emptying of the Divine Word in the incarnation is an expression of its own nature and self-identity. From all eternity, it has continually emptied itself through its receptive presence to the Father's will. Now, in the fullness of time, it empties itself before creation, humbling itself so that it can unite with humanity in order to transform it.

The Divine Word continues to be eternally spoken by the Father, even as it unites with a human body and soul. At the conception and birth of Jesus, the Word of God definitively enters our world and gazes upon the Father through the eyes of creation. As we ponder the mystery of the Christ child, it is important that we not lose sight of infinity's gaze upon the infinite, even as it has entered the limited boundaries of time and space. That gaze remains constant throughout Jesus' earthly sojourn — and beyond. The intensity of that gaze spills over into Jesus' human soul and nurtures in it a lasting bond with the Father. Through Jesus, the New Adam, that gaze also touches human nature. As it contemplates the depths of the Father's love, the

Eternal Word also contemplates our humanity. It does so not speculatively or abstractly but by pondering the very human body and soul to which it is united. This particular action has universal consequences, since the Word has bound itself to all of human nature, not merely a single historical manifestation of it.

At this moment of contemplation, we ponder the Incarnate Word as it opens itself up to the mystery of the Godhead. As we gaze upon the Christ child, we marvel not at its swaddling clothes and frail humanity, but at the mysterious depth of insight in which it shares. The infant Jesus is like an icon that opens one up to the beyond, to a deeper reality, to another realm of existence. The Word permeates this small child and beckons the beholder to ponder the Source from which it has come. As we gaze upon the child, we are gradually drawn into the world the Word has brought with it—its relationship with the Father and the Spirit. We sense the community of love to which they belong, and we recognize in our own hearts a deep desire to share in it.

This moment of contemplation of the Eternal Word helps us to appreciate even more the depths of God's love for humanity. The Trinity can be the perfect community of love only if it looks outside itself and seeks to bring others into its shared intimacy. The economic plan of creation, redemption, and sanctification reflects the diffusive nature of God's love and the desire to bring others into its fold. Realizing, however, that humanity could never come to God of its own accord, God chose to draw humanity to himself by entering our world and giving of himself completely, to the point of dying for us, so that he might become nourishment for us and a source of hope. When we ponder the Word in the God Incarnate, we see some of the first historical expressions of this self-diffusive love.

## LOOKING OUTWARD

The fourth and final moment of human contemplative activity ponders the Incarnate Word as it relates to humanity and the rest of creation. The Eternal Word entered our world not to visit us and then quickly depart, but to bind itself to us in a new and endearing way. It has taken on human nature in order to become one with us for all eternity. This new relationship between God and humanity opens up new possibilities for the rest of creation. In the incarnation, God's focus is not only on the redemption of humanity, but also on the creation of a new heaven and a new earth.

The incarnation represents a turning point in human history; humanity has been fundamentally changed because of Christ's birth. God now relates to us in a radically different way. Although the fundamental Creator-creature relationship remains the same, the focus has changed because the Creator has had the chance to view creation from within, giving us the hope of one day viewing the Divinity in a similar way. The union of the Divine Word to human nature marks the beginning of this mutual exchange of perspectives. The transformation of human nature took place at the Lord's resurrection and gave us the opportunity to be incorporated in that new humanity through baptism and our participation in the life of Christ's Body, the Church.

As we ponder the Word in its relationship to humanity and the world, we sense the uniqueness of what has taken place. In becoming flesh, the Word brings the infinite into the realm of the finite. That point of view marks a fundamental shift in the divine-human relationship. God is now everywhere in creation, not only by virtue of his sustaining power, but also by virtue of his personal presence. In the incarnation, the Word unites itself to humanity and becomes present to it in an intimate and personal way. The bond between the Eternal Word and humanity is so special that no model or metaphor in human experience comes close to describing it. It is more intimate than the bond of friendship, the parent-child relationship, or even ties between husband and wife, who become one flesh when they exchange the sacred vows of matrimony. The hypostatic union states that

God has become a man, while remaining both fully human and fully divine. This juxtaposition of opposites changes both God and humanity: the humanization of the divine creates the condition for the possibility of the divinization of the human. In the words of Athanasius of Alexandria: "God became human so that humanity might become divine."[14]

The gaze of the Word upon humanity allows humanity to look upon the divine in a new and different way. Jesus' relationship with the Father encompasses his whole being, the divine, as well as the human. Because of its relationship to the Word, his humanity was able to probe the depths of the Father's love for him and for the entire world. The Father's love for the world was mediated to Jesus' humanity through the external gaze of the Word, directed first toward Jesus' humanity and then through it to the rest of humanity and all creation. That gaze remained constant throughout Jesus' earthly life and through his passion, death, and resurrection. With his ascension into heaven, where he sits at the right hand of the Father, Jesus continues to gaze upon creation and work toward its ongoing transformation. As the Resurrected Lord, Jesus represents the firstfruits of the new creation. He rules over this new creation from the Father's right hand and constantly works to bring it to completion.

To see the various moments in our contemplation of the Eternal Word described above, we need only to examine a person in devout prayer before an icon such as Rublev's *The Holy Trinity*. Believers assert that an icon is like a window that can be viewed from both sides. On the other side of the icon, the Holy Trinity enjoys contemplative bliss in the intimacy of Father, his eternally spoken Word, and the loving bond between them (looking inward). On that side of the sacred, this perfect community of love peers through the icon's window to gaze upon the person praying (looking outward from within). On this side of the icon, the one praying simply gazes in silence upon the sacred image and allows three figures of Father, Son, and Spirit to become the focus of one's wordless prayer (looking inward from without). In this midst of this prayer, the gaze of the Trinity and the gaze of the person meet. As a result of this meeting, the light of divine grace flows from the heart of God into the heart of the person praying. The movement of grace in a person's life empowers him or her to delve beneath the appearance of things, look upon the world in a different light, and serve it in accordance with God's will (looking outward).

# Guidelines for Christian Living

As this description of praying before an icon indicates, the various moments of our contemplation of the Eternal Word are continuous with one another and lead to a more profound sense of the presence of God's Word in our lives and in the world. From these four moments of contemplation, we can also elicit a number of guidelines, all of which are interrelated and uniquely oriented toward the *telos* of the spiritual moral life in the new creation.

*We search out stillness.* As we make decisions about our lives, it is important for us to be in touch with the stillness of the Eternal Word that permeates not only our own consciousness but also all of creation. Doing so will give us a sense of our relatedness to each other and to the world around us. It will increase our sense of responsibility for the world and our part in it. Because we represent the created world becoming conscious of itself, it is essential that we use the gift of consciousness to tend the environment for the good of all and not for the selfish ends of a select few or a single generation.

*We engage in active listening.* The Eternal Word is the perfect expression of the Father and reflects that Word perfectly back to him. To do this, it must empty itself of all that is not of the Father and listen intently to what is being said. In a similar way, we must learn to empty ourselves before the moral challenges before us and listen carefully to what is happening. We must be able to enter a situation and reflect back perfectly what is being said. Only then will we be in a position to analyze the circumstances in which we find ourselves and respond in a manner worthy of our Christian vocation. The person who does not listen ultimately will not be heard.

*We recognize and accept our place in the universe.* When we contemplate the Eternal Word, we gradually come to recognize our smallness in the grand scheme of things. We understand that we are not the center of the world and must not act as though we were. Contemplating the Word fosters in us humility toward ourselves, others, God, and the world around us. It makes us conscious of the dignity of others, who also participate in the consciousness of the Word. It nurtures in us a respect for the world that is held in existence by the power of the Word.

*We value and form right relationships.* The Eternal Word is distinct from the Father and Spirit by virtue of its relationship to them. The Word cannot and does not exist outside of right relationship. In like manner, we must place the formation of right relationships at the forefront of our ethical concerns. To do so, we must be willing to examine the dysfunctional ways in which we relate (to ourselves, each other, institutions, the environment, God) and try to find ways of alleviating the tensions we find in our relationships. The goal we should be working toward is to have the relationships within the Trinity increasingly reflected in those we forge with others.

*We act as mediators.* As the Word mediates the world and all within it to the Father in the Spirit, so must we act as mediators wherever and whenever we discover broken relationships and a need for reconciliation. A mediator stands between dissimilar and, at times, even opposing sides in order to foster communion. A good mediator is respected and trusted by all sides. Any display of partiality has the potential to throw the entire process in disarray.

*We foster communion at various levels.* The Word exists in communion with the Father and the Spirit. It does so even as it turns its gaze toward humanity and the world. The communion in Godhead spills out into its creative, redemptive, and sanctifying mission. Much the same holds true for us. We too must strive to foster a spirit of communion with those around us. Doing so should be a priority in the moral choices we make and the course of action we take. We cannot give, however, what we do not possess. If we wish to foster communion in others and in the world around us, we must first do so in ourselves, with others, and in our relationship to God.

*We ponder our situation from afar.* The mystery of the incarnation was in the mind of God from all eternity, long before the birth of the Christ child in Bethlehem. Prior to committing itself to taking on human flesh, the Word pondered the situation from afar, planned a course of action, and put it into effect at the appropriate historical moment. We too must be able to step back from the complexity of the situation we find ourselves in and examine the larger picture surrounding our moral decisions before we commit ourselves to a particular course of action. When we ponder a moral dilemma in this way, we are often able to see significant factors that have a direct or indirect bearing on the choices before us.

*We seek to heal and transform.* As with the Word and its contemplative orientation toward action in the world, the criteria for our own involvement should be healing and transformation. When we ponder a particular situation, we must ask ourselves what is in need of healing and how it can be rectified and possibly even transformed. These questions are foundational for authentic Christian action. We must not merely acknowledge that there are questions or, worse yet, simply ignore them. We must ask the questions explicitly, or run the risk of promoting solutions to moral problems out of sync with the values of the grand, overarching narrative upon which our faith is based.

*We live in the service of others.* When contemplating the Eternal Word, we recognize that just as its inward gaze turns outward with the Father and the Spirit in the economic plan of creation, redemption, and sanctification, so too our contemplative gaze must turn outward at some point in service to others. Such service, however, must not take place without reason and forethought. Before acting, we should carefully consider the complex problems of the world around us so that we will be able to choose the course of action best suited to meet the challenges and circumstances of the moment. We acquire such practical wisdom by distancing ourselves from the issues before us in order to see the larger picture.

*We empathize with others and are involved in their lives.* As with the Word, we must also be willing to enter into the circumstances of the challenges we face and attempt to look at them from the inside out. Authentic Christian action cannot be done from the comfortable armchair of one's private study. To understand the world's problems, we need to engage them head-on and, when searching for solutions, we need to be willing to take into account even the slightest details. Just as God entered our world out of love for us, we must be willing to enter the world of those we serve in order to help them find genuine solutions to the challenging moral dilemmas of their day.

*We act out of love for others.* As with the Word, we must be motivated by a deep love for humanity that takes into account the dignity of the human person and the sacredness of the world we inhabit. The basis of these attitudes is that the human person has been shaped in the image and likeness of God and that God has left traces or vestiges of the divine as an imprint in the whole created world. This love is also manifested by a willingness to give of oneself for the sake of the other so that the other might be able to enjoy a more fulfilling life and a deeper, more intimate relationship with the Divine.

*We are committed to building up the kingdom.* When the Word entered our world, it changed the nature of the relationship between God and humanity for all time. It did not become flesh one moment and then leave the flesh in the next. Authentic Christian action in the world requires a commitment to building up the kingdom of God in the here and now. To do so, we must dedicate our entire lives to fostering the well-being of others on every level of their human makeup—the physical, emotional, intellectual, spiritual, and social. In the life of discipleship, commitment and discernment go hand in hand. Without them, our action in the world will be unreliable and out of focus.

*We recognize the uniqueness of our actions.* By entering our world, the Word establishes a distinctive relationship with humanity and the rest of creation. That relationship is unique and irreplaceable. In a similar way, it is important for us to remember that our action in the world possesses a singular and irreplaceable quality. All deliberated actions are similar in that they involve a concerted interplay of reason and will. They are unique, however, in that they take place at particular moments in time. We must recognize the importance of our action in the world. We find ourselves living at a particular point and space in time. However small or insignificant they may seem, our actions (or lack thereof) affect those around us and have consequence for the future. We must cherish our capacity for committed, reflective action and not take it lightly.

*We seek the infinite in the bounds of the finite.* In becoming flesh, the Word entered the limited confines of creation. This action brought the infinite into the realm of the finite and changed the nature and scope of our spiritual moral journey. From that moment on, it would not be humanity who would find God, but God who would find humanity. The finite would mediate the infinite to the human heart, and the human heart would be the dwelling place of God. Our finite human actions are more than isolated events in the directionless flow of time.

They have infinite consequences upon which the direction of our human journey hinges.

*Finally, we bring our actions to prayer.* We pray whenever we lift up our minds and hearts to God. To contemplate the Word in any of the ways we have delineated in the preceding pages requires God's help and initiative. Even when we ask for help, God has already initiated an action of grace that makes possible our request. When we contemplate the Word, it becomes clear that God initiates each of these various internal and external moments of contemplation. It also becomes evident that he initiates in us any desire we might have to carry on his work. Historically, the Word became flesh some 2,000 years ago. If we are to continue that work, we must foster an intimate relation with God that only prayer can provide.

The above guidelines for the spiritual moral life of the new creation in no way exhaust the insights to be gained from a contemplative meditation on the nature and action of the Eternal Word. Those listed above offer a good sense of how one of the most fundamental Christian doctrines can shape our spiritual moral sensibilities. The purpose of these guidelines is not to burden us with a list of impossible moral standards, but to point out some of the basic attitudes that contemplating the Word in an ongoing manner can instill in us over time. These guidelines are destined not for the moral manual or academic textbook, but the human heart. They are meant to be internalized ("made flesh," if you will) as fundamental attitudinal orientations of our spiritual moral lives. The way we do this is not merely by studying and applying them to concrete situations (however profitable that may be), but by actually contemplating the Eternal Word according to the fourfold plan described above. By pondering the mysterious features of the Word in this manner, perhaps by praying for a time before Rublev's holy icon, we will likely be more prone to seeing the way we must walk and the direction our lives should take.

# Conclusion

We can contemplate the Eternal Word only because it has first contemplated us in the eternal and mysterious depths of its divine knowledge. We can do so, because the Word's becoming flesh has inaugurated a new creation, one that has opened up new possibilities for us and permits us to relate to God in an entirely different way. Our contemplation of the Word is not an escape from the concerns of the present world, but a daring embrace of it that enables us to see our actions in a brighter, more revealing light. We contemplate the Word to understand why we are here and what it is we must do with our lives. We contemplate it in order to probe the mysteries of the beyond and to hear them echoing in the deepest recesses of our hearts. As Merton reminds us, contemplation "apprehends the Truth, not in distinct and clear-cut definitions but in the limpid obscurity of a single intuition that unites all dogmas in one simple Light, shining into the soul directly from God's eternity, without the medium of created concept, without the intervention of symbols or of language or the likeness of material things."[15]

This chapter has afforded us the opportunity to probe some of the most fundamental teachings of the Christian faith—the doctrines of the Trinity and the incarnation—in their relationship to the Eternal Word. The reflective, meditative nature of the discourse was chosen specifically to allow a contemplative appreciation of these mysteries of faith and to highlight the various processes involved in their internal and external relationships. Rublev's icon of *The Holy Trinity* helped us to understand just what happens when a person prays before an icon and what contemplating the Eternal Word means concretely in the lives of the faithful. In doing so, it enabled us to see that the spiritual and moral implications drawn from these processes have great relevance for us today as we search our faith for appropriate attitudes and values to guide us on our journey through life. The guidelines offered at the end of the chapter provide concrete markers against which we can measure our actions and determine whether they are consistent with the spiritual and moral implications of some of our most fundamental beliefs.

Every Christian doctrine has a variety of spiritual and moral ramifications associated with it. The purpose of this chapter has been to probe the doctrine of the Eternal Word in order to draw out these implications and bring them to the fore of our Catholic spiritual moral discourse. The nature of our probing has been meditative rather than analytical, one that would better dispose us to contemplating the mystery of the Word instead of deconstructing it through staid rational inquiry. The fruit of our reflection has been a list of basic Christian guidelines that should inform our outlook on life and inspire us to engage the world in ways befitting our Christian calling. For them to have any real lasting effect, however, these guidelines must themselves be meditated upon and internalized so that they might become deeply rooted in our conscious thought patterns and decision-making processes. Such internalization takes place most effectively when we open our hearts in quiet prayer and ponder the mysteries of God's Eternal Word in a dynamic relationship of reciprocal care and loving concern.

## CONTEMPLATING THE FACE OF CHRIST

1. Is the concept of an "Eternal Word" or a "Divine Logos" still relevant to today's world? Is it a concept easily understood? Does it make sense to people? Can you think of another idea or concept that would help to explain the mystery of God's revelation in Christ?

2. What does it mean to contemplate the Eternal Word? Is it possible for us to contemplate this Word by our own efforts? Do we need God's help to do so? Is it valid to speak of "natural" and "supernatural"

contemplation? If so, how would you describe the difference?

3. What is your reaction to the way the various moments of contemplation have been applied to the Eternal Word? Has this approach given you any deeper insights in this important mystery of the faith? If so, what are they and how would they describe them?

4. What do you think of the fifteen characteristics of the spiritual moral life that flow from contemplating the Eternal Word? Is there anything you would add to the list? Are there any you would remove? Are some on this list more important for the spiritual moral life than others?

## FOLLOWING THE PROMPTINGS OF THE SPIRIT

Find a quiet place away from the hustle and bustle of daily life where you can be alone for a few minutes. Go to church and kneel before the Blessed Sacrament; sit before a lit candle or an icon of Christ or the Holy Trinity in a small corner of your room; lie down on a peaceful spot beneath a shady tree. Wherever you go, try not to worry about the things you need to do. Try to put all thoughts out of your mind. Try instead to get in touch with the simple fact of your existence. Experience yourself as someone who exists, who has being, who simply is. Be grateful for this gift of existence. Ponder it. Embrace it. Rest in it. Look to its Source and bathe in its presence. By pondering your existence, you approach the threshold of Existence itself. Be silent before the Eternal Word as it speaks to your inner senses. Listen to it. Open your heart and allow yourself to be touched by it. Know that you exist only because you share in something greater than yourself.

# CHAPTER THREE

# Contemplating the Incarnate Word

> Men are called to form a single body, within an extraordinarily intimate divinization—and the Humanity of Jesus has been *chosen* to serve as the instrument for this unification in which the scattered cluster of all the fibers that make up the Universe is closely knit. In scripture, Christ appears to me as essentially invested with the power to give the World, in him, *its definitive form*. He has been consecrated for a cosmic function.
>
> Teilhard de Chardin[1]

Christianity hinges on the belief that God's Word became a man in the person of Jesus Christ. This singular belief is what separates the Christian faith from the other great world religions. Rather than humanity having to look for God, Christians believe that God has gone to great lengths to search out humanity. God did so by entering our world and becoming one of us. Although the incarnation took place in the historical personage of Jesus, our faith tells us that it had important consequences for humanity, the world, and the entire cosmos. It also has important implications for the spiritual moral life.

By becoming one of us, God initiated a process of transformation that oriented creation toward the divine in a unique and thoroughly innovative way. Divinized by its relationship to the Eternal Word, Christ's humanity represents the firstfruits of a new creation. Through baptism, we share in Christ's death and enter into that new creation through a process of divinization that leads to new life and a share in the resurrection.[2] By contemplating the mystery of the Incarnate Word, we gain insights into the dynamics of this transforming process and get a sense of the kind of intimate relationships in which God wishes us to share.

# Jesus Christ, God and Man

The Logos theology of John's Gospel summarizes very well the Church's understanding of the mystery of the incarnation: "And the Word became flesh and lived among us."[3] Rooted in the wisdom tradition of the Hebrew Scriptures and the Logos doctrine of classical Hellenistic thought, this late-first-century statement of antidocetic intent points to a new entrance of God's Word in the world.[4] In Jesus of Nazareth, this Word operated not by virtue of its creative and sustaining power (as with the rest of creation), but through its own personal Presence. The Word of God entered this world in a new and daring way: it lived among us, as one of us. As was said earlier, the incarnation represents a new creative moment in God's providential plan for humanity: God became human so that we might become divine. God's humanization, in other words, already anticipates humanity's ultimate divinization.[5]

In later centuries, the Church's teaching on the mystery of the incarnation was further refined in response to certain misconceptions about the relationship of Jesus of Nazareth to the Eternal Word, on the one hand, and to human nature and the material world, on the other. In its doctrinal formulations, the Church sought to avoid an overemphasis on either the human or the divine aspect of Christ's identity. At the first ecumenical councils —those of Nicaea (325), Constantinople (381), Ephesus (431), and Chalcedon (451)—it pronounced a series of solemn declarations to set forth its position clearly. The fundamental tenets of classical Christology go back to these important conciliar teachings. To understand them correctly, however, it is important to consider them in terms of what they were originally meant to negate. Against the Gnostics and Docetists, for example, the Church's emerging orthodoxy affirmed that the material world was good and that God did not merely appear in human form, but truly entered our world and became a man. Against the Arians, the fathers of Nicaea identified the Son not as a creature, but as consubstantial and one in Being with the Father. Against the Nestorians, the fathers of Ephesus identified the relationship between the human and divine in Christ as being not a mere moral or accidental unity, but an intrinsic union of natures. Against the Monophysites, the fathers of Chalcedon identified Christ as having two natures (one human, one divine) united hypostatically in one Divine Person. These christological teachings represent the Church's struggle to maintain the purity of its faith in the face of rationalist efforts designed to minimize the full mystery of Christ's identity. They convey particular truths about the meaning of this mystery and set themselves apart from dangerous distortions.[6]

What precisely does the Church say in its teaching on the Incarnate Word? It affirms that Jesus Christ is the Son of God, the Second Person of the Blessed Trinity, and that he has two natures, one human and one divine, which are intimately (that is, hypostatically) united. The Incarnate Word is a single Divine Person who is both human and divine. Jesus' divine nature relates to his human nature by means of an inner, substantial union that perfectly preserves his dual nature. Jesus is not the bearer of God, but is God himself; he is not a mere bearer of humanity, but is human himself. He is fully human and fully divine. This hypostatic union began at Jesus' conception, continues without interruption, and will never cease. According to Church teaching, each nature remains itself and is unmingled with the other. Each has its own natural will, intellect, and manner of operation.[7]

This brief summary of the classical Catholic teaching of the doctrine of the Incarnate Word does not even come close to fully expressing the mystery involved in the Word of God taking on human nature. Theological language by definition is limited and finite. There is an infinite gap between the truths expressed by these formulations and the divine mysteries they seek to express. The classical questions of Christology that concern the relationship between the human and divine in Christ are nothing more than an attempt to understand more deeply the precise meaning of the incarnation. The theological formulas used to express this relationship have changed and will continue to change with the growth in our perception of what it means to be human and of what it means to be divine. The challenge for modern Christology is to state the relationship between Christ's humanity and divinity in such a way that it will both remain faithful to past formulations and expand our present understanding of the meaning of the incarnation.[8] Whether or not such terms as *nature, hypostatic union,* even *person* are used has little relevance. However the idea is expressed, it is important for us to affirm that Christ entered this world completely, both fully human and fully divine. Contemplating the face of Jesus—be it as a child, adolescent, or adult—helps us to see the unity of his human and divine origins as essential to his identity. We cannot gaze into his eyes and ponder the mystery of his love for us without asking some very deep and probing questions about who he is, where he is from, and why he has come.

## Contemplating the Incarnate Word

Since no formula will ever exhaust the full meaning of the mystery of the incarnation, not even those set forth by the councils, the Church must always leave open the possibility that a new formulation at a future time may express the mystery more fully. Formulating the Church's teaching on the incarnation, however, is only the first step in a much larger process of assimilating the mystery of the Incarnate Word through human contemplation. Using the fourfold continuum outlined in chapter 1, we will now seek to demonstrate what contemplating the Incarnate Word reveals about the content and form of Catholic moral theology.

Before going through these different contemplative moments, however, you may want to first read and meditate upon one of the infancy narratives from the Gospels of Matthew and Luke.[9] If this suggestion is not possible at the moment, perhaps you could find an icon or picture of the nativity scene or, better yet, set up the manger to help you place yourself in the scene of Jesus' birth in Bethlehem. If even this option is not possible, then close your eyes and allow your imagination to re-create in your own mind the events of Jesus' coming into the world. The purpose of these suggestions is to provide you with some tangible way of connecting with the story of Jesus' birth, a day that we celebrate not only at Christmas, but whenever we experience anew the coming of Christ into our lives.

## LOOKING INWARD

The first moment of human contemplative activity involves the brisk and quiet stillness of the first Christmas morning. Like us, the Incarnate Word was born into this world as an infant. When we contemplate the newborn Christ child, we are pondering every newborn who comes into this world naked and in need of human nurturing. We are also getting in touch with our own entrance into life from the darkness of our mother's womb.

The Incarnate Word came into this world helpless and in need of someone to provide it all of the necessities of life. As we gaze upon the Christ child, we get in touch with our own vulnerabilities and need for others. The Christ child helps us to ponder the child within us, the one we once were and, in many ways, still are. The Christ child reminds us that we must always relate to God as children, for unless we become like them, we will never enter God's kingdom.[10] Contemplating the Incarnate Word helps us to become childlike. It reminds us both of our human origins and our human destiny. It gives us perspective on life about the things that really matter.

As we ponder the Christ child, we begin to sense that he is no ordinary child. It is hard for us to understand who he is and why he has such a hold over us. We feel we are in the presence of a great mystery. There is nothing strange or particularly out of the ordinary in his appearance: his helplessness and vulnerability echo in the cries of each newborn child; others are born every day into similar conditions of poverty and want. What makes him different? Who is this child before us? What does he want from us?

Somehow, we sense we are in the presence of the divine. In this child, God draws close to us as Emmanuel, "God is with us."[11] He desires to commune with us, to dwell among us, to live in our hearts. A feeling of wonder and awe swells within us. We desire, not only to gaze upon this child, but also to kneel and bow our heads before him. By his very appearance, this small child brings us closer to God. He leads us into God's presence and God into ours. It does so not through any profound and solemn gestures, but simply by being itself. This small, helpless child puts us in touch with both the vulnerability of life and its sanctity. It enables us to ponder life with different eyes, ones that can sense the presence of the eternal in the present moment and its ongoing birth in the deepest recesses of our hearts.

## LOOKING OUTWARD FROM WITHIN

The second moment of human contemplative activity involves entering into the mind-set of the Christ child as he looks out upon the world in all its freshness and noble grandeur. This action is a contemplative activity, for, not yet capable of discursive thought or critical analysis, a child is like a sponge before the world around it, receiving everything without question in a pre-rational, intuitive manner. The words of Hans Urs von Balthasar are helpful here: "The child is also a master of contemplation. He lies in the cradle or in a meadow and watches. He watches for hours. One does not know for certain what the child sees or whether he is consciously aware of the object on which his gaze rests. His contemplation hardly detaches itself from the identity which the subject and the object made up originally in God."[12] As we contemplate the Christ child, we enter into his own child-like contemplation of the world. In that contemplation, Christ's human nature mediates the world to the Divine Logos. God's Word interacts with the world through Christ's human nature and does not circumvent it. Although one represents a higher level of knowledge, the two work in harmony in a single acting subject.

A question obviously arises about the relationship between Christ's human and divine knowledge. Unique in the world, this relationship between the natural and supernatural spheres of Christ's knowledge has baffled theologians for centuries and will most likely continue to do so. Various models have been pro-posed—ranging anywhere from a declaration of Christ's human omniscience, on the one hand, to the affirmation of his human-ity's ignorance of any divine knowledge, on the other. All have something to offer and none completely satisfies. The full extent of Christ's knowledge remains a mystery. Because he was fully human and fully divine, it makes sense that some interaction would occur, although just how much and on what level we can-not be entirely sure.

One very plausible explanation comes from Gerald O'Collins, who emphasizes the intuited knowledge of the infi-nite in all human experience of the finite. If such is the case, Jesus in his divine capacity intuits the infinite in his finite human knowledge in a thoroughly unique and exceptional way: "In knowing what was finite and temporal through his human consciousness, he coexperienced the Infinite and Eternal as One to whom he stood in the intimate, personal relationship of son to Father. This coexperience of the Infinite differed from ours, inasmuch as it essentially involved the sense of a unique personal relationship to God whom Jesus named as 'Abba.'"[13] If such is the case, then our relationship with Christ promises to transform our limited intuited sense of the infinite already present within our finite knowledge. Christ came into this world to share with us his deeply intimate, personal relationship to the Father. We can experience this intimate bond of love only if we enter into relationship with the Incarnate Word; that is, Jesus, the Father's Son. When we contemplate the Incarnate Word in its openness to the finite world, we are given access to its intuition of the infinite upon which is based its personal relationship to the Father.

## LOOKING INWARD FROM WITHOUT

The third moment of human contemplative activity involves looking inward with the Incarnate Word on itself as it embarks on its redemptive mission in the world. The activity of the Incarnate Word in the world does not disrupt its inward communion with the Father. Jesus continues to contemplate the Father inwardly even as he engages others in outward activity. As we contemplate the Incarnate Word from this vantage point, we begin to understand what it means to cultivate a contemplative attitude toward life. Contemplation and action are not opposing or countervailing forces, but different dimensions of human activity meant to act in concert in the service of others. Contemplation, one might say, reaches its perfection in loving action. "True solitude," as Thomas Merton asserts, "is the solitude of charity, which 'seeketh not her own.'"[14]

Jesus was able to remain immersed in a deep, intimate contemplation of the Father even as he went about the normal activities of everyday life. Although he sought out special times and places to delve even more deeply into the mystery of his Father's love, the bond of communion that he shared with the Father was not subject to the vicissitudes of earthly circumstance. Jesus' intuition of the infinite in the midst of his finite daily activities gave him deep confidence in his filial relationship to the Father. This experience of Divine Sonship was his most fundamental attitude of mind, one that shaped his outlook on life and the way he chose to relate to others. Jesus wanted nothing more than to share his relationship with the Father with others. By contemplating the Incarnate Word in this way, we see the contours of Jesus' relationship with the Father and long to share in it.

As we continue to contemplate the Incarnate Word, we gradually get in touch with God's call for us. Jesus' action in the world does not get in the way of his relationship with the Father, but provides the conditions under which it is tested and strengthened. In a similar way, we must look upon our own activity in the world as an opportunity for deepening our relationship to God. God the Father calls us to a deep, intimate relationship with the Divine. This relationship is possible by virtue of our being members of Christ's Body. By looking inward at the Incarnate Word's relationship with the Father as it engages in activity in the world, we get a sense of the kind of dual orientations that we ourselves must strive to possess: one toward the divine; the other toward the world. As we mature in the spiritual moral life, these dual orientations will eventually merge in a single current of contemplative action. Until it takes place, however, we can look with hope to Jesus, the Incarnate Word, as someone who shows us the way to the Father even as he engages the world in a life of caring service.

## LOOKING OUTWARD

The fourth moment of human contemplative activity involves pondering the mystery of the Incarnate Word as it carries out its redemptive mission in the world. Jesus Christ is "the way, and the truth, and the life";[15] in him, contemplation and action are one, just as two streams flow together to form a single river. Jesus' action in the world both flows from his contemplation and leads back to it. He contemplates as he acts and acts as he contemplates. This close unity stems from his capacity to see the infinite within the finite and the finite within the infinite. He does so because he himself is a unique "coincidence of opposites."[16] He is divine and human, God and man, Word made flesh.

When we ponder Jesus as he acts in the world, we see him at the height of contemplation. In him, contemplation leads to action and finds its fulfillment in it. Jesus' contemplative action manifested itself in a life of loving service. It showed itself in his teachings and in his miraculous cures, in his love for the poor and marginalized, and eventually in his laying down his life for his friends. Jesus lived and died for others. He also rose for others. The purpose of his action in the world was to heal the human heart so that it once more could contemplate the divine, commune with it, and share in its mission. Jesus came to us so that we might once again be able to enjoy God's friendship. He contemplates us so that we might be able to contemplate him. We do so through our participation in his life, made possible through the sacraments.

These sacred rituals effect what they signify and, as such, are a continuation of Jesus' contemplative activity in the world today. As actions of Christ, they incorporate us into his Body and become our own. In this way, our actions become Jesus' actions; our thoughts, his thoughts; our words, his words. This is especially true when we gather at Eucharist. There, the Word who became flesh for our sake enters our midst once more, this time in the form of bread and wine. At Eucharist, we engage in a great act of remembering, one that carries us into the timeless mystery of Jesus' passion, death, and resurrection. The Eucharist is a contemplative action on both Jesus' part and our own. Through it, God ponders us from within by becoming our food and drink. Nourished in this way, we contemplate the Lord dwelling not only in our midst, but now also within us. With the Lord present to us in this intimate way, we contemplate the humanity we share with him and live in the hope of its final transformation.[17]

# Guidelines for Christian Living

As the above reflections indicate, contemplating the Incarnate Word touches upon and has important ramifications for nearly every aspect of the Christian faith. Be that as it may, it should come as no surprise that those contemplating the Incarnate Word have a special place in their heart for a small cave in Bethlehem, where the Virgin Mary gave birth to a son and named him Jesus, "Emmanuel, which means, 'God is with us.'"[18] Down through the centuries, Christians the world over have pondered the meaning of this newborn child for their lives. To guide their reflections, they pondered the infancy narratives and used their imaginations to place themselves in the scene.

In the year 1224, using livestock and real people, Francis of Assisi created the first nativity scene in a small cave on the outskirts of the Italian town of Greccio. People came from far and wide to see his re-creation of Jesus' birth, and it soon became a favorite way for the faithful to celebrate the coming of Christ into the world. Francis's goal was to give the simple people of his day a concrete way of connecting with the Christmas story so that the love it represents would overcome the power of darkness in their hearts. His reenactment of the first Christmas underscores the close connection between spirituality and morality, contemplation and action, prayer and daily life.

In a similar way, the various moments of contemplation presented in this chapter have concrete implications for Christian living. The union of these activities brings a new dimension to our outlook on action in the world. Rather than focusing on the quantity of our actions, we gradually become more concerned with their quality. As Merton puts it: "Our being is not to be enriched merely by activity or experience as such. Everything depends on the quality of our acts and our experiences. A multitude of badly performed actions and of experiences only half-lived exhausts and depletes our being."[19] These moments of contemplation relating to the mystery of the Incarnate Word promote the high quality of human action in a variety of ways. While in no way exhaustive, the following list of guidelines identifies many of the characteristics that a stance of contemplative action toward the world has for the quality of the spiritual moral life.

*We have a deep respect for creation and the material world.* The mystery of the incarnation affirms the fundamental goodness of the visible world. For the Word of God to take on human nature, it was necessary for it to come in close contact with matter and the dimensions of time and space. By entering human history and choosing to dwell among us as a man, God's Word entered into a new relationship with creation. As a result, our relationship with Jesus has ramifications for the way we relate to the world around us. Our attitudes toward matter and the environment, for example, should reflect the same attitudes that led God's Word to embrace the material world in such a loving and selfless manner. If our attitudes do not, then we should ask God to help us overcome the prejudices that keep us from treating our environment with the dignity and respect it deserves.

*We cultivate a sense of wonder about the world around us.* Jesus blessed the children who came to him and said that the kingdom of heaven belonged to such as them.[20] Children have the capacity to take in the world and simply stand in wonder at it. Their curiosity knows no bounds. They wish to explore their environment, not analyze it. They can easily lose themselves in the present moment and lose all track of time. When contemplating the Incarnate Word, we are challenged to get back in touch with the childlike gaze that fills us with wonder of the nature of things. The capacity to live in wonder of life is necessary for contemplative action in the world. Without it, we lose the sense of life's underlying mystery and easily lose sight of how important it is for our actions to be in tune with it.

*We strive to integrate the contemplative and action-oriented dimensions of our lives.* Jesus brought his relationship to the Father into everything he did. There was no dichotomy between his contemplative communion with the Father and his contemplative action in the world. There was a circular relationship between them that gave him the strength to overcome his fears and embrace the Father's will with free and total willingness. In our own lives, we must strive to bring our contemplation to action—and vice versa. We must strive to contemplate as we act and to act as we contemplate. In doing so, our actions become an offering to God and an extension of God's presence in the particular boundaries of the space and time in which we live.

*We use appropriate and fitting means to achieve our intended goals.* God's Word could have entered our world in any one of a number of ways (for example, in a vision, as an angel, as a full-grown man or woman). He chose to be born a child, however, because he wished to share in our human experience to the fullest extent possible. His incarnation in the womb of the Virgin Mary was the most fitting and appropriate way of doing so. For God, it was not simply a matter of achieving a specific goal, but of doing so in an appropriate way. When we contemplate the Incarnate Word, we recognize that we too must be conscious that the ends of our actions are correct and that the means we choose to achieve them are in line with our dignity as human beings created in the image and likeness of God.

*We foster a respect for the human person.* God's Word entered our world and became one of us. In doing so, human nature was elevated and was brought into a new relationship with the divine. Christ is the New Adam. He invites us to take off the old self and to put on the New Man.[21] We do so by opening our hearts to the power of Christ's Spirit. In this way, the power of

God's grace can transform each of us into a member of the new humanity and the new creation ushered in by Christ. For this reason, we must have respect for every human person. Each person has a heart that can receive and reflect to others the infinite love manifested in Christ's passion, death, and resurrection. Lack of respect for human beings indicates a lack of respect for God, who embraced humanity as if it were a part of his own self.

*We contemplate and deeply respect the various stages of human life.* As noted above, God's Word did not have to enter our world the way it did. It could have chosen a much more dramatic entry on the stage of human affairs. Its decision to enter in the normal way demonstrates its deep embrace of the human journey and its desire to accompany us at every step of the way. By entering our world as a child, God's Word blesses the human journey and makes it sacred. Because of this decision, we must revere human life at all its stages, from the first moment of conception to the final breath of life. We must also respect the various processes of human growth and development. In our interactions with others, we must strive to meet people where they are and do our best to lead them into the next stage in their human development.

*We recognize the various levels of human sinfulness.* God's Word entered our world to elevate humanity. Before he could do so, however, he also had to heal it of its sinful tendencies. Sin has infected our human situation on three levels: the personal, the social, and the universal.[22] Often referred to as "original sin" or the "sin of human origins," the universal level is the most deeply rooted in humanity. Through his passion, death, and resurrection, Jesus freed humanity of its slavery to this fundamental flaw in our nature. Although the consequences of this universal level of sin are still present in our lives, our redemption in Christ assures us that it no longer has a lasting claim on us. Christ's transforming and elevating grace is at work in our lives and in the lives of the people we serve.

*We seek to enter the world of others.* God's love is self-diffusive. The Father manifested his love for all by sending his only begotten Son into the world in order to give of himself to others, become food and nourishment for them, and offer them a source of hope. As followers of Christ, we must seek to act in a similar way. We must strive to enter the world of those around us, give of ourselves to them, become nourishment for them, and offer them a source of hope. We can follow in this path of discipleship, however, only if we ask Jesus himself for the help to do so. Left to our own resources, we are incapable of loving the way Christ loves. If we live in communion with him, however, he will work through us and draw others to him. We live in communion with Christ by opening our hearts in prayer each day and inviting him to dwell within our hearts.

*We forge bonds of solidarity with others.* Jesus' solidarity with the Father moved him to enter into bonds of friendship and solidarity with others. He did so by seeking people out, caring for them, and proclaiming God's nearness to them. He did so by making their plight his own. Jesus considered love of God and love of neighbor closely related; for him, it was impossible to have one without the other. In a similar way, we cannot pretend to profess our love for God and then simply ignore those in need. Doing so would be disrespectful to God, to those we treat in this manner, and to our own human dignity. As Jesus' followers, we must strive to live in staunch solidarity with others. His presence in our lives bids us to bear that presence to others through our thoughts, words, and actions.

*We dedicate ourselves to promoting the common good.* God's Word entered our world for the sake of all humanity. The Incarnate Word's mission was not merely to teach and heal those particular individuals with whom he came in contact during his time on earth, but the redemption of the entire human race. The mystery of the incarnation has a decidedly universal focus, one that seeks to take into account not merely individual needs but those of humanity as a whole. For us, this larger perspective translates into an appreciation of the importance of identifying and promoting the common good of society, of humanity in general, and of the world as a whole. We do this by getting in touch with the common humanity that we share with everyone we meet and by working for the establishment of a truly just society. *We reach out to the weak and vulnerable, to those in society who are poor and marginalized.* The Incarnate Word entered this world helpless and vulnerable, much like the rest of us. The difference with Jesus, however, is that he never lost sight of his human fragility and fundamental need for God. He always maintained an attitude of childlike dependence on Abba, his Father in heaven,[23] an attitude that was nurtured by contemplation of the Father and his recognition of his utter need for God. This recognition led him to reach out to others in need, especially the poor and marginalized. Deeply in tune with his own fragile human condition, he could see his own vulnerability reflected in others and acted accordingly. As followers of Jesus, we must be in touch with our own frailties so that we can understand the vulnerabilities of others and reach out to them in times of need.

*We seek to live in fellowship with God at all times.* Jesus, the Incarnate Word, represents God's desire to live in fellowship with humanity. The process of divine self-emptying that made this possible represents a divine gift to humanity, one for which we must be forever grateful. When we contemplate the Incarnate Word, we stand in awe of the magnitude of this gift and in gratitude for how it affects our relationship with the Divinity. The incarnation of God's Word made living in fellowship with God once again possible for us. To cherish this gift, we must strive to walk humbly with God at all times. Doing so should be the major focus of our life, one that we take into consideration as we engage others and the world around us.

*We strive to seek God in all events and circumstances.* Jesus was Emmanuel, God with us. When contemplating the Incarnate

Word, we gradually come to a deeper realization of God's presence in our lives and in the world around us. Although it is often difficult to sense the Divine Presence, the Catholic faith teaches that God is everywhere and is at work in all situations. By living lives of contemplated action, we actively look for God's presence in the people we meet and the situations we face from day to day. We look for his presence by cultivating a listening and discerning heart, one which is able to look beneath appearances and to recognize the true needs of those we are seeking to serve. By seeking God in all things, we affirm God's love for creation and sovereignty over human history. We also profess God's personal love for us and hope in God's providential plan for our lives.

*We celebrate the sacrament of the present moment.* The Incarnate Word came into the world to help us find our way back to God. In Jesus, the Divinity entered our world, so that we could live in intimacy with it. Our contemplative activity in the world must allow that process of divinization to take shape. Being in communion with Jesus helps us to discover the eternal in the present moment. It enables us to dwell in the eternal, just as the eternal dwells at this very moment in the depths of our hearts. Through Jesus, we learn to appreciate the sacramental significance of our actions. We see that they are not mere transitory events, but expressions of self that shape who we are and affect our destiny both as individuals and as a people.[24]

*Finally, we live in the hope of our full and final transformation in Christ.* God's Word entered our world to redeem it and to create humanity anew. Although the Resurrected Christ is the firstborn of this new world and new humanity, redemption will not manifest its full effects until the final judgment of the living and the dead at the consummation of time. Until then, we must walk humbly before our God and live in the hope of his unending love and mercy for us. We must also ask for the help we need to cooperate with the process of divinization initiated by Christ as it slowly does its work in us and transforms us into the persons

God wants us to become. A life of mature and ongoing contemplative action is a life lived in hope. Such hope intensifies our desire for God and draws us closer to our heart's desire.

Although the above guidelines do not exhaust the implications of what contemplating the Incarnate Word might have for the spiritual moral life, they do offer a general sense of the kind of attitudes and values we are to bring to our actions as we engage the world for the sake of the Gospel. Like Francis's re-creation and dramatization of the first Christmas, they offer an important reminder of the challenging spiritual moral formation that we all must undergo in order to be effective witnesses to Christ and his message. As such, they provide us with a glimpse of an authentic Christian vision and ethic that has direct consequences for the contemplative actions of Christians in both society and the world at large.

# Conclusion

It took the Church several centuries to formulate its doctrine on the mystery of the Incarnate Word. It did so in order to clarify its position against those who had offered minimalist or exaggerated interpretations of Jesus' nature, identity, and mission. To counteract these tendencies, the Church convened a series of ecumenical councils that, in time, identified Jesus as a single Divine Person with distinct yet hypostatically related human and divine natures. Through this unique "coincidence of opposites,"[25] the Church affirmed Jesus as fully human and fully divine. He was the mystery of the Incarnate Word: Son of God and son of Mary, the New Adam and the Resurrected Lord, the Redeemer of humanity and King of the new creation.

Despite the directness and seeming coherence of these claims, we should still not forget that the primary focus of theological inquiry during the development of the dogma of the incarnation was not mere intellectual clarity, but a profound sapiential knowledge of the divine mysteries. The teachings of the Church sought to help the Christian community probe the mysteries of the faith and to offer its members a solid base from which they could offer up heartfelt prayers to God. These teachings were not abstract intellectual truths, but pregnant symbols of faith that spoke to the deepest recesses of the heart. When contemplated in this way, they conveyed a vast nexus of spiritual moral insights that were intrinsically oriented toward an intimate knowledge of the divine.

In addition to subjecting the doctrinal formulations of the Incarnate Word to careful, intellectual scrutiny, we must also ponder the mystery revealed in the quiet depths of our hearts. If the theological community in recent years has focused almost exclusively on a critical analysis of the doctrines of the faith, perhaps the time has come for it to shift its focus by emphasizing the importance of contemplating them for the spiritual moral values they impart.

In this chapter, we have contemplated the mystery of the Incarnate Word in a way that reveals some of the most important spiritual moral insights of the Catholic faith. Inspired by the Gospel infancy narratives and by imaginative meditations on the nativity scene, we have gazed upon the Christ child and pondered how, even now, he lives and moves and has his Being as God's Eternal Child and Incarnate Son. From this contemplative focus, I have drawn out a number of important spiritual and moral values that shape our outlook toward Christian action in the world and influence our concrete decisions in our everyday lives.

## CONTEMPLATING THE FACE OF CHRIST

1. Why is the mystery of the incarnation so essential to the Christian faith? Should adhering to this belief be a test for orthodoxy? In your opinion, do most Christians firmly believe in this doctrine or

do they give mere notional assent to it? What can be done to present this teaching to the sensitivities of today's believers?

2. Do you believe that the Church's teaching on the incarnation is the final word on this important mystery of the Christian faith? Do you think there is room for other formulations of the relation between the human and divine in the person of Jesus Christ? If so, how should these affect the traditional formulation?

3. Should contemplating the mystery of the Incarnate Word change a person's perception of it? Should it change a person's perception of the Church's doctrinal formulations? Should contemplating the mystery of the Incarnate Word change a person's perception of God? Should it change a person's perception of humanity?

4. How does contemplating the mystery of the Incarnate Word affect the spiritual moral life? Do you agree with the fifteen implications listed near the end of the chapter? Is there anything you would like to add to the list? Is there anything you would like to remove?

## FOLLOWING THE PROMPTINGS OF THE SPIRIT

Children have a unique way of contemplating themselves and the world around them. Think back to the time of your childhood and try to remember the things that captivated your imagination and filled you with wonder. Are these memories easy or difficult to recall? Do you enjoy remembering them? Is there anything you would rather not remember? Now try to ponder what took hold of Jesus' imagination as a child and what filled *him* with wonder when he first entered our world. Stay with him as he grows and matures, looks, and ponders the world's weakness and brokenness. Dream with him as he considers what must be done to heal it and make it whole. Walk with him as he sets out to fulfill his Father's will. Jesus entered our world as a child of God and never lost sight of it. What can you do to recapture your childhood innocence? What do you need to let go of? Whom do you need to forgive? What do you need to do? Remember that Jesus is God's only begotten Son and wants you to share in his eternal childhood. He entered our world so that we could one day enter his. Ask him to help you to get in touch with the child that you once were and, to a great extent, still remain.

# CHAPTER FOUR

# Contemplating the Life and Ministry of Christ

Jesus does not fit into any category. Neither ancient nor modern, nor Old Testament categories are adequate to understand him. He is unique. He is and remains a mystery. He himself does little to illuminate this mystery. He is not interested in himself at all. He is interested in only one thing, but interested in it totally: God's coming rule in love. He is interested in God and human beings, in God's history with human beings. That is his mission. We get closer to the mystery of his person only when we look into that mission. The theological perspective is the only one which does not falsify the person and work of Jesus.

Walter Kasper[1]

Jesus lived and ministered for the coming of the kingdom. He entered our world to proclaim the nearness of God's rule of love and paid for it with his life. When we think of Jesus' redemptive action, it is important for us not to overlook the period between his birth and the paschal mystery. His entire earthly life, both hidden and public, was part of the total offering of self that began in the incarnation and reached its culmination in his death on the cross and glorious resurrection from the dead.

In this chapter, we will ponder what the narrative of Jesus' life and ministry—as told for centuries, popularly received, and ingrained in the Christian imagination—reveals about his purpose and self-identity. In doing so, we hope to gain a better understanding of what he sought to accomplish for us and why he gave up everything to see it through. This narrative tells us that Jesus' life was defined by his mission and reveals to us the true meaning of discipleship. It tells us that he was like us in all things, yet never fell short of carrying out the will of his Father in heaven. It encourages us to walk in his way and reminds us that to do so means to live in humble recognition of our limitations and in eager anticipation for the coming of the kingdom. This kingdom is still to come, yet because of Jesus' life and ministry it is also already reflected in our midst.[2]

## Jesus' Divine Sonship

Have you ever wondered what it would be like to encounter Jesus when he walked the earth? How would you react to him? What would you say to him? If you knew nothing of his subsequent history, do you think you would be a disciple of his? Would you look upon him with suspicion as did many of the pious Jewish leaders of his day? Who would you say he was?

There have been many attempts over the years to ascertain Jesus' true identity. Volumes have been written on the quest for the historical Jesus and the relationship between the Jesus of history and the Christ of faith. These attempts have employed different methods and achieved varying degrees of success. While many can point to genuine insights about his calling, identity, and mission, none can claim to have presented a definitive picture of this elusive historical figure. The person and character of Jesus, moreover, have sometimes been shaped to fit the categories used to measure him, thus making him more an anachronistic projection from another time than an authentic reflection of his own.[3]

Through all these years of historical critical speculation, the Church has held steadfast to its conviction about the fundamental continuity between the Divine Logos, the historical Jesus, and the Risen Lord. It bases this claim not on scholarly biblical criticism, which it values as only one of several helpful tools for the study of God's Word, but on its understanding of divine revelation as flowing from scripture and tradition and as safeguarded by the ongoing interpretation of the Church's magisterium.[4] When seen in this light, Divine Sonship becomes the unifying thread and source of personal identity of Jesus the Christ. As the Creed itself asserts: "We believe in one Lord Jesus Christ, the only Son of God, eternally begotten of the Father."[5]

According to Catholic belief, there is one and only one Son of God, who became man, suffered and died for our sins, rose from the dead in a transformed, glorified state, and ascended into heaven to sit at the Father's right hand. A genuinely Catholic consideration of Jesus' life and ministry cannot divorce itself from this fundamental claim about Jesus' personal identity. Ultimately rooted in the experience and witness of the apostles and the faith of the early Church, this assertion affirms that time and eternity, the human and divine, history and faith, have somehow converged in the person of the historical figure known as Jesus of Nazareth. As such, it grounds Jesus in space and time, yet also carries him beyond them. The strictures of critical historical inquiry cannot verify this assertion, since it is a revelatory claim rooted in faith. As such, it comes from beyond history and ultimately transcends it.[6]

Jesus' identity as the Son of God provides us with an important key with which to understand his life and mission. He lived and acted with a purpose hidden in the depths of his intimate relationship with the Father. This relationship influenced his conscious thoughts and unconscious desires and lay behind his hidden life in Nazareth, his public ministry in Galilee and Judea, and ultimately his sacrifice of self on Golgotha, just outside Jerusalem's city walls. It also lay behind those moments of solitude with God that he sought in desert wastelands and on lonely mountaintops, as well as in those dramatic symbolic actions of baptism and table fellowship that marked the beginning and end of his public ministry. Everything Jesus did pointed to the Father and to the coming of God's reign. As Prophet, he boldly proclaimed that God's kingdom was to come, yet was somehow already in his midst. As High Priest of the new covenant, he gave himself up to death and opened the way to salvation. As King, he established a new universal order governed by the love of enemies, the practice of the Beatitudes, and the rule of selfless giving.[7]

Jesus' Divine Sonship has important repercussions for his relationship with us. By entering our world, living among us, giving himself to us, and dying for us, he made his relationship with the Father available to us. As a result, he no longer calls us slaves, but friends.[8] On Easter morning, he rose as the New Adam, the firstborn of the new creation. We rose with him as members of his Body and have now become the Father's adopted sons and daughters.[9] Even the prodigals among us receive the same loving and compassionate attention as God's only begotten Son, if we are but willing to accept it.[10] For Jesus, the reign of God was all about establishing a new order of relationships based on the disclosure of God's unending love for humanity. The Eternal Word became a man, lived among us, taught us, healed us, and died for us in order to make us sons and daughters of God. In doing so, he now relates to us as his brothers and sisters and asks us to do likewise in our relations with him and one another.[11]

In his life and ministry, Jesus fostered an ever-growing circle of kingdom-oriented relationships. He would not allow rejection, at times even by those close to him, to deter him from his goal. What began at Bethlehem with his incarnation in his mother's womb was, at Nazareth, nurtured in his immediate family life with Joseph, his adoptive father, and in his life among his kinfolk, neighbors, and fellow villagers. These relationships from Jesus' so-called hidden life were eventually extended to those in his public ministry in Galilee and Judea to include all people, especially the poor and oppressed, outcasts, and those in need of physical and spiritual healing. After his passion, death, and resurrection, they were then offered to everyone who ever lived and ever would live.[12]

Jesus' relationship with the Father ties all these facets of Jesus' life together. What once existed solely between the Father and his only begotten Son was freely given to humanity through Mary's grace-filled *fiat* and had repercussions for Jesus' hidden life and public ministry. What once was hidden was progressively made public and then universal. What was deep in the depths of the Father's love took flesh in the womb of Mary, became visible at Bethlehem, grew and matured in Nazareth, became public in Jesus' ministry, and universal in Jesus' paschal mystery. Jesus' life and ministry were all about establishing the relationships of the kingdom. Wherever and whenever they appear, the kingdom that he preached enters our midst and extends that circle of relationships even further.[13]

# Contemplating Jesus' Life and Ministry

The doctrine of Divine Sonship reconciles the Jesus of history with the Christ of faith and provides the point of continuity between the Logos, the incarnation, and the Risen Lord. It lies at the center of Jesus' self-identity and has great importance for our attempt to understand his life and ministry. Contemplating certain aspects of Jesus' earthly life—his communion with the Father, his contemplative attitude, his sense of purpose, his total self-offering—brings to the surface many important insights into the Christian spiritual moral life. If nothing else, it reminds us that "the true saint is not one who has become convinced that he himself is holy, but one who is overwhelmed by the realization that God, and God alone, is holy."[14] Jesus' life and ministry point to the one thing that matters: God alone is holy, and he alone can make us holy.

## LOOKING INWARD

Jesus' life is traditionally divided into his so-called hidden time at Nazareth and his public ministry in Galilee and Judea. The first includes his infancy, childhood, adolescence, early adulthood, and growth to manhood. The second begins roughly at the age of thirty with his baptism in the waters of the Jordan by John the Baptist and continues for approximately three years where he leads the life of an itinerant preacher, teacher, and miracle worker.

It is generally agreed that Jesus' hidden life extends from his early life to his baptism by John in the Jordan, while his public ministry begins with his baptism and continues until the events in Jerusalem that lead to his passion and death. Jesus' birth and baptism define his hidden life; his baptism and celebration of his Last Supper, his public ministry. Both his hidden and public lives, moreover, can be said to converge in the terrible events of his passion and death, a truth that is appropriately symbolized by the presence of his mother Mary and his beloved disciple at the foot of the cross, who represent figures coming respectively from his hidden and public lives.[15]

When contemplating Jesus' life and ministry, it is important to remember at the very outset that both dimensions of his life, the hidden and the public, were always intimately connected. The roots of his public ministry were already present in his hidden life, just as he carried his hidden life within him wherever he went during his public ministry. It is also important to remember that each of these dimensions of Jesus' life and ministry flowed out of and, in many respects, remained hidden in his relationship with his heavenly Father. Both his hidden life in Nazareth and his public ministry in Galilee and Judea were equally "hidden" in his relationship to his Father and his identity as Divine Son, and at every stage of his earthly life, Jesus' actions were influenced by his relationship to his heavenly Father.

Although it would be impossible to determine the depth of his consciousness of this relationship, we may surmise that he became increasingly aware of it as his mind matured and as he went through the various stages of human development. We may also suppose that his growing awareness of his Divine Sonship manifested itself in a deep experience of communion with the Father and a profound capacity to contemplate the divine. Jesus, we might say, lived entirely out of his relationship of communion with the Father and a contemplative attitude toward the divine that permeated his entire outlook. When we view his life and ministry in this way, we see that everything his did—both in private and in public—flowed from his relationship to the Father. Our contemplative gaze upon Jesus reveals communion with the Father and contemplation of the Father as the primary means through which he lived his life and sought to extend the relationships of the kingdom to others. As he lived his earthly life, in other words, he never stopped living in communion with and contemplating the divine. As a result, he was able to look upon people and events as his heavenly Father saw them and for what they were destined to become.[16]

## LOOKING OUTWARD FROM WITHIN

Jesus lived his life and went about his public ministry not only while in deep, intimate communion with his heavenly Father, but also while contemplating the people and events surrounding him. His marked and profound contemplative attitude toward life flowed from his relationship of Sonship to the Father and is closely related to his premeditated actions for the world's redemption. This activity had both internal and external dimensions in the life of the Son. Before its implementation in the mysteries of the incarnation and Jesus' life, death, and resurrection, it was already present in the mind of God as a providential design for the establishment of a new creation.

A plan for the world's redemption existed in God's mind from all eternity and continued to exist even as Jesus carried out this activity in time and space. Jesus' contemplative gaze toward the people and events surrounding him flowed from his being in contact with this divine plan and his understanding of it as being an expression of the Father's will. Although it is difficult (indeed, next to impossible) to ascertain the extent to which Jesus was humanly aware of the various intricacies of this plan, we may reasonably conclude that it manifested itself, in the very least, in a deep sense of trust in the Father's love and the promptings of the Spirit that moved him. It was out of this deep sense of trust that Jesus was able to contemplate the world around him and implement God's redemptive plan for humanity.

Our ongoing contemplation of Jesus' life and ministry reveals a man deeply rooted in his relationship to the Father and who allowed that relationship to shape his outlook toward the world and motivations for acting in it. We see someone who was continually in touch with the personal ground of his existence and who was able to sustain an ongoing contemplative gaze upon the world that eventually gave rise to the liberating actions that filled his entire life and ministry. We see someone who truly was in the world, but not of it, someone whose relationship with the Father would not allow him to cave in to pressures, prejudices, and ideologies surrounding him. We see someone who sensed the eternal in the present moment and who acted in order to help others do the same.

Our contemplation of Jesus' life and ministry also sees someone whose contemplation moves him to compassionate and loving action in the world around him. Jesus' relationship with the Father will not allow him to contemplate the world from afar without getting involved in it and taking an active role in its affairs. Jesus is the "contemplative in action" par excellence. His ministry is not a mere consequence of his contemplative activity, but an actual extension of it. It flows from his relationship to his heavenly Father and his loving gaze upon the world into which he has freely chosen to live, preach, teach, and heal.[17]

## LOOKING INWARD FROM WITHOUT

Jesus' relationship with the Father and his contemplative outlook toward the world gave him a deep sense of purpose and mission. In the next phase of our contemplation of Jesus' life and ministry, we notice that his actions are connected by an underlying sense of resolve. His thoughts, words, and actions are interrelated and connected by an underlying unity. He speaks to us in order to move our hearts. He touches us in order to make us whole. He reaches out to us in order to bring us closer to the Father. As the Word of God made flesh, Jesus' actions are the actions of the Father. His thoughts, words, and actions are God's revelation, the announcement of a new beginning, a new creation, a new humanity. His mission is to bring the Good News of the inbreaking of God's reign of love.

Jesus' life and mission embody this reign. Everything he says and does reflects the Father's love for a world gone awry. His life and mission flow from his relationship to the Father and his contemplative outlook on life. He comes to call us into communion with him so that he might lead us back to the Father and enjoy with him the fullness of life. As Jesus acts in the world, he sanctifies it. The air he breathes is cleansed. The ground he treads becomes hallowed. The people he encounters are never the same. Because God has walked upon it, the world has become a different place. The entire world has become the Holy Land—and we, God's Holy People.

Jesus remains centered in the midst of much activity. There is a calmness about him that never goes away, a still point from which all else radiates. He sustains this inner calm even when he is in the throes of intense missionary activity. His actions are not separated from his contemplative gaze but flow from it, just as a ray of light flows from its source. Jesus' actions ultimately flow from the will of the Father. The words, "Your kingdom come, Your will be done," come from his heart, not merely his lips, and reflect his deep experience of communion with the Father.[18] Jesus' life was his mission—and vice versa. His seeks out the Father's will at all times and in all circumstances. He carries it out without ever thinking of himself, seeking only to serve, rather than be served.

Our contemplation of Jesus' life and ministry reveals someone whose words and actions are authentic and correspond fully to his stated purpose. If holiness is to will the one thing necessary, to be entirely focused on carrying out the Father's will, then Jesus was not only holy, but Holiness itself. His life and ministry were a life and ministry of sanctifying, of "making holy." He did so not merely through his preaching, teaching, and miracles, but by living a life that was entirely grounded in the Father's love. Jesus experienced the depths of the Father's love for him at the very core of his existence. His life and ministry flow out of that experience and he seeks to share it with others.[19]

## LOOKING OUTWARD

Jesus' life and actions speak for themselves. In his hidden life at Nazareth, he lived the ordinary life of a Jew in first-century Palestine. He knew the warmth and security of a family's love, which protected him, first as an infant and then as a boy, from the harsh realities of living in an occupied land and from those who would harm him and might even wish to take his life. He grew up with an extended family of kinsmen and local villagers, who gave him a sense of belonging to a greater whole—a people blessed by God and chosen to enter into covenant with him. As an adolescent, he understood the value of both work and play. He helped with the chores and learned his father's trade. He kept the Sabbath and learned the words of prophets and the tales of his ancestors preserved in the Torah.

Jesus' hidden life was valuable in itself, for it put him in touch with the experience of human growth and development. It was also a time of preparation for his public ministry, during which time he preached a radical new message to the people of Israel. The kingdom of God was at hand. God had visited his people and had come to establish with them a new covenant, one forged not in the blood of animal sacrifice, but in Jesus' total offering of self. His death on Calvary must be understood in the context of his life and ministry. It was not an idiosyncratic event disconnected from all that came before, but the culmination of everything he lived and stood for. Jesus' experience of communion with the Father impressed upon him a deeply contemplative outlook toward life that propelled him into a life of selfless giving. This total offering of self is a part of Jesus' self-identity. It flows from his relationship to the Father and manifests itself in his maturation, in his life and ministry, and in his sacrificial death.

Our contemplation of Jesus' life and ministry reveals him as a man entirely dedicated to others. His life of selfless giving manifests itself in his deep desire to carry out his Father's will so that the experience of communion known to him might be extended to others. His contemplative outlook on life leads him to a life of preaching, teaching, and healing. It also leads him to provide concrete signs of God's mysterious action and loving presence in the world. Most notably, these include immersion in the waters of baptism, which is a mark of his entrance into the new covenant,[20] and his offering of bread and wine at his Last Supper with his disciples,[21] a foreshadowing of his sacrificial death, a symbol of his abiding presence, and a foretaste of the heavenly banquet. By emptying himself into these and other sacramental actions, Jesus acts where and whenever they are performed, thereby extending his life and ministry through time and space. Through them, he raises his life and ministry to a new level, for he now lives, moves, and breathes through the members of his Mystical Body. In doing so, he has brought his contemplative gaze full circle. His communion with the Father, his contemplation of the world, his sense of messianic mission, his total offering of self, his sacramental actions—all converge in our lives as we carry out his mandate to follow and serve. The lives we now live are not our own, for Christ lives within us.[22]

## Guidelines for Christian Living

Jesus' life and ministry always point to the one who sent him. "The teaching and miracles of Christ," as Thomas Merton puts it, "were not meant simply to draw the attention of men to a doctrine and a set of practices. They were meant to focus our attention upon God himself revealed in the person of Jesus Christ."[23] When contemplating Jesus' life and ministry, we begin to understand that his thoughts and actions flow from his intimate relationship with the Father and that it was for this reason that they bore fruit and did not return in vain.

It should come as no surprise to us, therefore, that contemplating Jesus' life and ministry also has clear implications for Christian living. At the outset of this chapter, you were asked to imagine what it would be like to encounter Jesus face-to-face when he walked the earth. You were also asked to think about how you would react to him and what you would say to him and how you would respond to the question, "Who do you say that I am?" Without exhausting the possibilities, the following guidelines draw out some of the implications of Jesus' life and ministry for our own. They presuppose, however, that your answer to the question of Jesus' identity resembles that of the apostle Peter: "You are the Messiah...the Son of the living God."[24]

*We acknowledge and celebrate the personal ground of our existence.* Jesus' relationship with the Father reminds us that a personal Presence lies behind all of reality and is with us at each moment of our lives. This Presence brings the universe into being and sustains it from one moment to the next. Although we are but a small part of this creation, we are deeply cherished by this personal Presence, even beloved. Nothing else in all of creation except for us bears its image and likeness.[25] Through his life and mission, Jesus puts us in touch with this Presence, this personal ground of our existence, and teaches us to relate to it as a child relates to a loving father. Jesus acknowledges and celebrates the Father's love by seeking to carry out his will. He asks us to follow his example and do the same.

*We live in communion with the Father and seek to share this relationship with others.* Jesus' life and mission flow from his relationship with the Father. From this experience of intimate love and communion flows his deep sense of purpose. Jesus derives his identity from his relationship with the Father and enters our world to share that identity with us. His life and mission cannot be understood apart from this relationship and his deep desire to share this relationship with us. Because of Jesus' life and mission, the Father adopts us as his own sons and daughters, and he embraces us in his paternal embrace. As a result, we not only relate to God in a new and different way, but we also take on duties and responsibilities we never had before. Jesus' mission and purpose now become our own. With him, we live in communion with the Father and invite others to join in.

*We seek to view everything that happens to us in the light of our relationship to the Father.* Jesus' relationship to the Father shaped his entire outlook on life. It gave him a deep desire to do the Father's will at all times and in all circumstances. He viewed everything that happened to him in light of this relationship and made his decisions accordingly. Because we are members of Jesus' Body and share in his relationship to the Father, we too look upon everything that happens to us in light of this precious bond. We act out of our relationship with the Father and seek to do only what we discern to be in accordance with his will. Like Jesus, we seek not our own interests, but the interests of the Father. We actively pursue those interests for the building up of God's kingdom.

*We contemplate the people and events around us.* Our relationship with the Father and the experience of communion flowing from it fosters in us a contemplative outlook on life. We extend a contemplative gaze upon those we meet and the circumstances in which we find ourselves. This gaze helps us to keep things in perspective and to remember what is most important. It helps us to step back from life and to value it at a deeper level. It helps us to ponder our actions beforehand so that we do not act impulsively or with little forethought. Our contemplative outlook on life flows from our experience of communion with the Father, which comes to us through the Son and in the Spirit. Our actions flow from our contemplation, and our contemplation is rooted in our experience of God.

*We listen to others and ponder what they say.* Jesus was intent on doing the Father's will. For this reason, he needed to listen to the silence within him and around him so that he could hear the Father's voice and properly discern what it was saying. Jesus' capacity to listen intently to the voice of his Father also affected his relations with others. Because he listened deeply to what others were saying, he was authentically present to them and able to discern their real needs, those behind the words and often left unspoken. As members of his Body, we seek to be present to those we serve in such a way that we truly listen to them and respond to their genuine needs. Listening in prayer helps us to listen in ministry. Both are necessary in discerning and carrying out the Father's will.

*We offer ourselves in service to others.* Jesus' total self-offering flows from his relationship to the Father and his contemplative gaze on the world. It is an expression of the Father's will and explains every dimension of his life and mission. Jesus was a man for others; he came to serve, not to be served. He humbled himself by becoming one of us and living among us. He did so that he might draw us to himself and reestablish our relationship to the Father. Our relationship to the Father moves us to do the same. Our contemplative gaze upon the world moves us to compassion and inspires us to empty ourselves in a life of service for others. We put the interests of others before ourselves and take concrete action to alleviate the world from suffering and lead others to the Father's love.

*We view our lives in terms of mission.* Jesus' life was closely identified with his mission. He preached, taught, cured, and forgave: all were personal expressions that flowed from his intimate relationship with his Father. He identified with and considered himself One with his Father. Everything he did flowed from this experience of personal communion and expressed itself in his mission. As members of Christ's Body, we too are asked to view our lives in terms of mission. Although not all of us are called to spread the Good News as missionaries in foreign lands, we are all called to mission, wherever we find ourselves. Jesus extends his mission through space and time through the members of his Body. We are his eyes and ears, his lips and tongue, his arms and legs, his hands and feet that carry his message of love for all to hear.

*We forge bonds of communion and solidarity with others.* Jesus' mission and purpose in life was to give humanity the opportunity to enter into communion with his Father. He did this by his total offering of self that expressed itself in a life of service to others. We too are called to build bonds of communion and solidarity with those we serve. Like Jesus, we do so by entering their worlds and giving ourselves to them, to the point that we become nourishment for them, and a source of hope. Whenever we establish such bonds with others, the kingdom of God enters our midst in a concrete, palpable way. We succeed in transforming a part of the world into a haven of divine love. The more we extend Christ's kingdom of love to others, the more prepared we will be for his long-awaited return.

*We mission in and through community.* Very early in his public ministry Jesus gathered around him twelve apostles and a much larger group known as his disciples.[26] They followed him and learned from him as he made his way through the countryside and the various towns and villages of Galilee and Judea. At one point, he sent them out two by two to cure the sick, cast out demons, and spread his message of the coming of the kingdom.[27] This communal dimension of the disciples' mission was meant to give them human support and to lend a watchful eye so that no one strayed from the Master's teaching. Jesus' disciples today also need to be aware of the important communal dimension of their ministry. "Going it alone" runs counter to Jesus' message and may well prove dangerous and even counterproductive. If we truly wish to follow Jesus and partake in his mission, it is important for us do so in community and as community.

*We live simply and without clutter.* Jesus had few possessions and claimed to have no place to lay his head.[28] He was not tied down by possessions and was thus able to travel about lightly and in complete freedom. His simple lifestyle enabled him to focus completely on his mission. He was detached from property and possessions so that he could dedicate himself completely to proclaiming the coming of God's reign. He became poor not for the sake of being poor, but so that his message would resonate with our common humanity. His disciples today are also called to live simply and without clutter. Doing so will help us to put things in perspective and to see their true value. It will enable us to cling more tightly to what truly matters and to minister to others without looking for reward or recompense.

*We find time for prayer.* Even Jesus, who was in constant union with Father, found it necessary to set himself apart and pray. Doing so gave him the opportunity to rest and regain his strength after his extended missionary efforts. He retreated into the desert for forty days and nights before he began his public ministry.[29] At various other times during his ministry, he went up a mountain or found a deserted place to be alone with the Father and commune with him in solitude.[30] These moments of quiet retreat were an intimate part of Jesus' life and mission. They enabled him to explore the depths of his relationship with the Father and reinvigorated him for what lay ahead. We too need to find moments in our lives to get away and be nourished by God through prayer and reflection. Such moments can help us to grow in our relationship with God and deepen our dedication to our mission.

*We read the scriptures as a way of discerning the Father's will for us.* Jesus spoke not like the scribes and Pharisees, but with authority.[31] He used simple language, parables, and examples from everyday life to touch the hearts of his hearers. He chose his words wisely and used them to draw others close. He knew when to challenge and when to console. He knew when to begin and when to end. He knew what to say and how to say it for the sake of the kingdom. Whenever we read the scriptures, Jesus speaks to us with the same authority and sense of immediacy. Through our slow, meditative reading of the Word of God, we sense the Lord's Spirit moving our hearts in the midst of the silence and revealing to us the Father's will. We read the scriptures to listen to God's Word to us and to discern its meaning and relevance for our lives.

*We value purity of heart and seek to foster it in others.* In his Sermon on the Mount, Jesus blessed those who were pure of heart and said that they would see God.[32] The pure of heart are the single-hearted, those who see their goal and focus all their energies on it until they reach it. Jesus himself possessed this important quality of heart. His steadfast and single-hearted devotion to his mission set him apart from the religious leaders of his day. He was totally focused on doing his Father's will and would not rest until he finished what he set out to accomplish. Like him, we too are called to be single-hearted in our lives and dealings with others. We will accomplish the mission that God has set out for us only if we keep our hands to the plow and refuse to look back.[33] We will see God in the kingdom to come only if we intently keep our eyes on him in the here and now.

*We find words that will touch people's hearts and draw them closer to Christ.* Once we discover the Lord's will for us, we too must seek to find the words that will move people's hearts and lead them along the way of conversion. To discover these words we need to ponder, reflect, think, and, most of all, pray. The words we speak must be authentic. They must come from the heart. They must reflect our experience of communion with Christ and our deep desire to know and carry out the Father's will. These words must be simple, clear, and direct. They must speak the ordinary language of the men and women of our time. Their purpose is to offer the people we serve a glimpse of the Father's love for them. They are meant to entice people, to draw them on, to encourage them to get in touch with and actively seek the deepest yearnings of their hearts.

*We receive the sacraments and view them as unique opportunities to encounter Christ and be touched by his grace.* When he walked the earth, Jesus lived a historical life. Seated at the right hand of the Father, he now lives a mystical life through the members of his Body.[34] The sacraments are the visible mysteries of faith he has given us that we might remain in close contact with him. They are actions of Christ that render worship to the Father through him and in the Spirit. The sacraments mediate Christ's love to us and remind us that Jesus has promised to be with us until the end of time. They are historical signs of our transcendent destiny to be with Christ in the presence of the Father. We are divinized by them and empowered to carry on Christ's mission and purpose.

Contemplating Jesus' life and ministry has great relevance for our own lives. The above guidelines highlight just some of the attitudes and values reflected of his hidden and public lives that should also be reflected in ours. These authentic qualities of mind and heart are not of our own making, but come to us as gifts. We acquire them not by external imitation, but as a result of entering into communion with Jesus so that we might share in his intimate relationship with the Father. To live in communion with Jesus is to share in his life and ministry—and to call them our own. We do so with him living within us and using us, as members of his Body, to proclaim the coming of his kingdom.

# Conclusion

Jesus' life and ministry are a continuation of an eternal process of self-offering that manifests itself historically in the mystery of the incarnation and culminates in the mystery of his passion, death, and resurrection. His life and ministry tie together his entrance into the world and his departure from it to form a single redemptive narrative that touches the human heart and offers it healing and fullness of life. Those who contemplate this narrative and enter into its dramatic warp and woof do not emerge from it unchanged. They find their own lives reflected in it and receive from it a deep sense of purpose and dedication to mission.

When we contemplate Jesus' life and ministry, we discover a person entirely focused on doing the will of his heavenly Father. This sense of single-hearted purpose unites his hidden life in Nazareth with his public ministry in Galilee and Judea. It shows us someone who listened intently to God's Word as revealed in the scriptures and who saw it fully reflected in his heart. Throughout his life, Jesus drew his strength and identity from the Father and was interested only in the coming of God's rule of love. He lived and ministered to this end—and eventually gave his life for it.

Jesus' life and ministry also offer us helpful guidelines for Christian living. As we ponder them, we find the way that we too should walk. "Follow me," Jesus said to his first disciples.[35] Although only a relative few people were ever given the privilege of meeting Jesus face-to-face when he walked the roads of ancient Palestine, the call of discipleship extends now to all and resonates deep within anyone who receives Jesus' invitation with an open, yearning, and listening heart. The story of Jesus' life and ministry challenges, cajoles, motivates, and fascinates us. As we reflect upon his words and actions, we sense a call to view our lives and relationships in an entirely different way. We identify with Jesus' communion with the Father and his contemplative outlook on the life. We are moved by his sense of purpose and wholehearted dedication to his mission. We desire to follow him, to "go and do likewise." What we have received from him, we now seek to understand and offer to others.

## CONTEMPLATING THE FACE OF CHRIST

1. What do you personally believe about the particulars of Jesus' life and ministry? How did you arrive at these convictions? Are there any inconsistencies or contradictions in them? Do they need to be revised in any way? Do they take into account the insights of the historical critical method? Do they provide for the theological insights of the Catholic faith?

2. Do you agree that Jesus derived his identity from his Father and that this relationship permeated his entire life and ministry? How would you describe this relationship? What affect did this relationship have on his private life in Nazareth? What affect did it have on his public ministry in Galilee and Judea? What significance does this relationship have for your own life?

3. Do you agree that Jesus' relationship to the Father expressed itself in a contemplative outlook toward life? What characterizes such an outlook? Can you point to concrete examples of this outlook in his

life and ministry? Is this outlook something that he also wishes you to share? If so, what steps can you take to foster such an outlook in your own life?

4. Do you make it a point to contemplate Jesus' life and ministry? Do you think you should? How often do you do so? Would you recommend it to others? What benefits have you derived from it? Has it helped you in your own life and ministry? To what extent has it helped you to foster a contemplative outlook in your own life?

## FOLLOWING THE PROMPTINGS OF THE SPIRIT

Take a few minutes at the end of the day and try to remember all that you did. Try to be as specific as possible. What were its bright spots and dark moments? With whom did you talk, eat, and pray? Did you have a difficult time with anyone? Did you travel or stay put? What work did you do? Did you find any time for rest? Were you able to spend time with your family? How would you describe your priorities for the day? After a short while, try to imagine a typical day in the life and ministry of Jesus. Follow him as he makes his way from one village to the next. Watch him as he encounters people in need and cares for them. Listen to him as he speaks and teaches from the depths of his heart. Walk with him. Talk with him. Eat with him. Pray with him. Rest with him. After you have done so for a while, take all the events of the day that just passed and place them in Jesus' hands. Ask forgiveness for the times you shut him out of your life and activities. Ask him to help you to follow him more closely. Invite him to accompany you at every moment of the coming day.

# CHAPTER FIVE

# Contemplating the Cross of Christ

To know the Cross is not merely to know our own sufferings. For the Cross is the sign of salvation, and no man is
saved by his own sufferings. To know the Cross is to know
that we are saved by the sufferings of Christ; more, it is to
know the love of Christ Who underwent suffering and
death in order to save us. It is, then, to know Christ. For to
know His love is not merely to know the story of His love,
but to experience in our spirit that we are loved by Him,
and that in His love the Father manifests His own love for
us, through His Spirit poured forth into our hearts. To
know all this is to understand something of the Cross, that
is: to know Christ. This explains the connection between
suffering and contemplation. For contemplation is simply
the penetration, by divine wisdom, into the mystery of
God's love, in the passion and resurrection of Jesus Christ.

Thomas Merton, *No Man Is an Island*[1]

Someone once said: "There is a cross in God before the wood is
seen on Calvary."[2] This statement places the cross in the very
depths of God's being and views Jesus' death on Calvary as an act
of compassion that reveals the very nature of the divine. "God is
love," the First Letter of John tells us.[3] The cross is the ultimate
expression of this divine love; it flows from God's heart and
touches us in the midst of our own suffering.

In this chapter, we will contemplate Jesus' passion and death and examine what they mean for the Christian life. When we ponder Jesus hanging on the cross, we come face-to-face with the God who loves us and suffers with us. The words of Merton introducing this chapter remind us that to contemplate is to penetrate the mystery of God's love and to grasp through Divine Wisdom that the way of the cross ultimately leads to fullness of life. Jesus fostered this fullness throughout his life and came to see that love was stronger than death. By letting go of his life and placing himself with complete trust in the hands of his heavenly Father, he overcame death and brought humanity to new heights. Because of Jesus, our humanity now touches the very heart of the divine. His passion and death reveal the power of God's love to cast out the darkness from our hearts and fill them with its burning and penetrating light. We affirm this power in our daily lives every time we make a simple act of faith, even one as common as blessing ourselves with the Sign of the Cross.

## Jesus' Passion and Death

One way of gaining insight into the meaning of Jesus' suffering and death is to look at his "seven utterances" from the cross, commonly called his Seven Last Words, that are found in the passion narratives of the Gospels of Luke, John, and Matthew.[4] Although there is no way of determining their actual chronological sequence and even though the historical authenticity of some has been brought into question, the Catholic faithful have, for centuries, listened to these words and allowed them to penetrate their hearts. In doing so, they have let the death of their Lord touch them in a very deep and personal way. Jesus' Seven Last Words have deep roots in Catholic literature, art, and devotion and are typically presented in the following order.

## "FATHER, FORGIVE THEM; FOR THEY DO NOT KNOW WHAT THEY ARE DOING"[5]

In his first words from the cross, Jesus turns to his Father in prayer and intercedes for us on our behalf. He does so to ask the Lord for something that we are unable to ask for ourselves. Because of our ignorance and inability to accept responsibility for our own actions, Jesus gathers us into his heart and presents our plea to the Father. He stands in our place and closely aligns our destiny with his. In doing so, he makes us members of his Body and allows his dying words spoken from the cross so long ago to resound deep within the fabric of our being even today.

## "TRULY I TELL YOU, TODAY YOU WILL BE WITH ME IN PARADISE"[6]

Jesus' words to the good thief inspire hope and confidence. The scene reminds us that it is never too late to open our hearts to God and seek forgiveness. Filled with remorse, one of the thieves crucified with Jesus turns to him and humbly asks to be remembered when he enters his kingdom. His words reveal both a change of heart and the life-giving act of faith. How fitting it is that someone should come to believe at the very hour of Jesus' death! Without this same fundamental conversion of heart, none of us would be able to enter the kingdom. On the other hand, perhaps it would be better to say that, without it, the kingdom would not be able to enter us. "Paradise for God," we are often told, "is to dwell in the human heart."[7]

## "WOMAN, HERE IS YOUR SON.... HERE IS YOUR MOTHER"[8]

Looking down from the cross, having been suspended between two worlds, nearing the threshold of death, Jesus looks upon his mother and his beloved disciple and entrusts them to each other's care. His words to them show the kingdom for which he lived and died taking root in the world. Because of his actions, human relationships now have new possibilities. Our closest bonds are no longer those of blood, but those formed in faith and in the loving desire to do God's will. The Spirit forges these new family bonds, and Jesus' commandment of love becomes the primary means by which they are shared.

## "MY GOD, MY GOD, WHY HAVE YOU FORSAKEN ME?"[9]

Uttering these words from the cross, Jesus reveals himself to us as a man of deep prayer. His words of lamentation come from a heart already broken by human ingratitude and soon to be pierced by a soldier's lance. That heart opens in a cry of desperation, looking for consolation from a God who now seems strangely absent. Jesus cries out to God and questions him: "Why have you forsaken me?" Each of us has probably asked or will ask this question at some point in our sojourn through life. It is a question about suffering and death, about the meaning of life and ultimately about our need for God.

## "I AM THIRSTY"[10]

These words contain many layers of meaning. Those who ponder them soon recognize the depth of Jesus' longing for humanity. He wants more than just water to wet his tongue and to ease his pain. His thirst represents, at the same time, both God's yearning for humanity and humanity's yearning for God. In Jesus, the two have become inseparable. As we draw closer to death, we come face-to-face with our thirsts. We look to Jesus and recognize that he has gone before us. By uniting ourselves to him, his thirst becomes our thirst; and our thirst, his.

## "IT IS FINISHED"[11]

Jesus speaks of the end of his suffering and the completion of his mission. They are words of courage from someone intent on carrying out the Father's will, regardless of the consequences. They are words of expectant understanding, enduring patience, and steadfast perseverance uttered at the end of a life violently cut short. As he speaks, Jesus is about to breathe his last and release his Spirit into his Father's hands. His mission is accomplished, and yet only begun. There is always one more heart to open, one more spirit to move, one more soul to touch.

## "FATHER, INTO YOUR HANDS I COMMEND MY SPIRIT"[12]

Jesus' final words from the cross are a prayer from the heart addressed to Abba, his Father in heaven. His Father is also our Father. We too are encouraged to turn to him with deep heartfelt prayers in times of need, especially at our hour of death. We should not hesitate to do so and need not be afraid. Jesus has already spoken to him on our behalf: he has carried us in his heart and given us to his Father; he asks us to open our hearts and do the same.

Jesus' last words from the cross fill us with awe at the depths of his love for God and humanity. He emptied himself so that he could be filled with our humanity and offer himself to his Father in our place. The cross was the means by which he demonstrated the extent of his love. He was not intimidated by its brutality or frightened by its deadly grasp. He faced his executioners with hopeful resignation; his imminent end, with quiet resolve. The cross brought Jesus to the threshold of death, where he experienced the full impact of humanity's willful separation from God.

Over the centuries, Jesus' words from the cross have become a mainstay of Catholic literature, art, music, and devotion—and in recent years they have even made it to the silver screen. The uniqueness of these words, however, lies not merely in their power to move the human heart, but in their ability to transform it. After Jesus uttered these words, his heart was pierced with a lance and blood and water was seen to flow from his side,[13] symbols of the close connection between his sacrificial death and the regenerating waters of baptism. Jesus' last words draw us into the mystery of his passion and, as a result, into the infinite ocean of mercy that flows from his side. Contemplating these words leads us inexorably to a deeper encounter and understanding of Jesus' paschal mystery.

# Contemplating Jesus' Passion and Death

Jesus' passion and death represent the climax of his process of self-emptying. By delivering himself into the hands of his enemies, he demonstrated complete trust in the Father's love and a willingness to embrace it with complete abandon. This act of obedience reveals both his close bond with the Father and his deep love for humanity. In keeping with the approach we have taken in previous chapters, we will now seek to demonstrate what contemplating Jesus' suffering and death tells us specifically about the Christian spiritual moral life.

## LOOKING INWARD

To begin with, Jesus' passion and death go far beyond the historical events that took place on Golgotha. While those events represent the climax of Jesus' self-emptying, they do not exhaust the depths of his love. That love was manifested in the incarnation and throughout Jesus' earthly life. It was also present in the loving relationship that he shared with the Father from all eternity. Jesus' redemptive love—of which his death by crucifixion was the ultimate expression—flows from and is intimately related to his filial relationship with the Father. The Son enters our world, gives himself completely to us to the point of dying for us, and becomes our nourishment and source of hope, precisely because it is what the Father wills.

This loving relationship with the Father motivates the Son to restore humanity's broken relationship with the divine. When seen in this light, Jesus' death on the cross is just as much an expression of his love for the Father as it is for humanity. "The Father and I are one,"[14] Jesus tells us in John's Gospel. This unity penetrates the very fabric of his being and makes him completely of one mind and heart with the Father. Jesus communes with the Father and acts out of this close relationship. Because of it, he listens intently to what the Father tells him and thoroughly understands it. Jesus' internal obedience to the Father consists in a constant reoccurrence of this twofold movement.

The word *obedience* has its origins in the Latin word *audire*, which means "to listen." Because he lives in such close communion with the Father, Jesus has a unique capacity to hear what the Father is saying to him. His capacity to listen flows from his deep love for prayer. When alone at prayer and in the midst of deep solitude, Jesus not only reveals his own innermost thoughts and desires to the Father, but also hears in the deepest recesses of his heart the concrete expression of the Father's will for him. The Father's will resounds within Jesus' heart, because he himself is God's Word. In listening to the Father's Word, he thus ponders himself. When the Word became man, this pondering of self also enabled Jesus to hear the cry of humanity deep within his heart. Jesus' suffering and death are intimately tied to his steadfast and enduring capacity to hear the will of the Father and to identify with our frail, broken humanity. Through such listening, he comes to understand his role in the Father's providential plan.

Listening ultimately leads to understanding. Jesus' capacity to focus his complete attention on the Father's will leads him to moments of deep insight. He communes with the Father so closely and so intimately that he comes to view the world around him through the eyes of the Father. As a result, Jesus not only listens to the Father, but also grasps his meaning and intention. He sees the world and everything in it from a divine perspective. He understands the truth about things, their inherent weaknesses, and the limitations that flow from their created nature. Although it is impossible to tell to what extent Jesus could articulate this understanding, the Gospels depict him time and again as someone with a deep sense of the Father's providential plan for humanity and the special role he was to play in it. They also present him as a teacher and healer, as someone who sought to free people from the oppression of ignorance and disease and to make them fully alive with the Spirit of the Living God.

## LOOKING OUTWARD FROM WITHIN

Jesus not only listens to and understands the Father, but also is oriented toward action. He is moved to respond out of love for both the Father and the world. "The Word became flesh and lived among us," the Gospel of John tells us.[15] In the person of Jesus, divine compassion has become visible for all to see.

When we contemplate Jesus' passion, we see his desire to give up his life freely so that we might be delivered from our bondage to sin and death and be able to share once more in an intimate relationship with the divine. Jesus' suffering and death represent the final act of the Son's obedience to the Father. The Word became flesh, not only in order to dwell among us, but also to suffer and die for us. This stage of our contemplation of Jesus' passion helps us to see it as an active manifestation of God's providential plan, which is rooted in the Father's relationship to the Son and the Son's relationship to the Father. Through the cross, humanity is lifted up into this intimate, compassionate relationship. Jesus' suffering and death bring meaning to our own and inspire us to trust in the Father's unconditional love.

When we ponder the passion, there is a temptation for us to think solely in terms of what *is being done* to Jesus. His suffering can be thought of as a very passive affair, as something that he must receive and undergo. While there is some truth to such a scenario, we should not forget the active and courageous way in which he freely embraced his impending death. He did not try to escape the road to Golgotha, but walked it freely and openly. He set his face firmly on Jerusalem and knew that within its gates, he would be handed over to the Roman authorities and put to death. Jesus suffered death, but did so by means of an active embrace. His passion was passive, yet also active. He accepted it without complaint and, by welcoming it as the Father's will, made it thoroughly his own.

Once Jesus' passion is seen as a free and active embrace of the Father's will, its importance for our redemption takes on deeper significance. While it is true that the entire Christ event—from the incarnation, to Jesus' earthly life and ministry, to his passion and death, to his resurrection and ascension into heaven—concerns God's redemptive plan for humanity, the sacrifice of Calvary contributes something unique. On the cross, Jesus lifts up our humanity with his own and sacrifices (literally, "makes holy") the death we all one day will undergo.[16] He makes death holy because he is both human and divine. The redemptive action begun at the incarnation (the divine becoming human) reaches its climax when Jesus is lifted up on the cross (the divine-and-human suffering the ravages of death), and its fulfillment at the resurrection (the divine-and-human overcoming death).

When seen in this light, the well-known salvific principle—"God became human so that humanity might become divine"—embraces every dimension of the Christ event.[17] What Jesus accomplishes through his loving self-emptying on Golgotha, however, is unique in that it brings the process of dying into the sphere of the sacred. Only after humanity dies with Jesus on the cross can it hope to rise with him on Easter morning. To redeem humanity, therefore, Jesus had to enter into the fullness of human experience: from birth to death—and everything in between. By carrying our humanity with him along the way, he gives us the opportunity, not only to overcome death by making it holy, but also to share in the fullness of life that he himself shares as he sits at the right hand of the Father.

## LOOKING INWARD FROM WITHOUT

Firmly grounded in his relationship to the Father and oriented toward the action of loving self-emptying as a result, the Son sets out to implement a program of action that ultimately brings about humanity's redemption. Although God in its three Persons always and everywhere acts as one, we normally attribute the act of creation to the Father, that of redemption to the Son, and that of humanity's sanctification to the Holy Spirit. For this reason, God's redemptive activity is normally associated with the Son.

Once the Son has assumed our broken humanity, his suffering and death become a recurring theme throughout the Gospels. In the Gospels of Matthew, Mark and Luke, for example, Jesus often refers to his approaching passion and death during his public ministry.[18] These references can be taken not only as omens of events to come but also as signs that, on some level, Jesus is already experiencing the weight of his cross. Similarly, in the Gospels of Matthew, Luke, and John, some of Jesus' postresurrection appearances appear to be woven into earlier chapters dealing with his earthly ministry, the implication being that the various aspects of the Christ event are intimately related and must be understood in the context of one another.[19] In Byzantine iconography, moreover, Jesus' passion and death are often represented in the nativity scene, with the child's manger resembling an altar, even a tomb, and its swaddling clothes, a burial cloth. The implication of such imagery is that the Son of God was born to die and, in dying, "makes holy" and therefore redeems the whole of human life.[20]

If Jesus' passion and death are somehow foreshadowed and even anticipated at his birth and during his public ministry, it must also be remembered that there comes a time in his life when he sets his sights toward Jerusalem and has a very good sense of what will take place there. Jesus sets out toward Jerusalem—the heart of Jewish life, culture, and worship—to proclaim his message of the imminent coming of God's reign. He enters triumphantly through the city gates, widely acclaimed as a prophet and Son of David,[21] and within a short while disrupts the routine proceedings at the Temple by expelling the merchants and money-changers.[22] Within a few days, he is betrayed by one of the Twelve,[23] denied by another,[24] and abandoned by nearly all the rest.[25] In the process, he is handed over to the religious and political authorities, brought up on charges of promoting religious and political unrest, and condemned to death by Pilate.[26]

At this stage of our contemplation of Jesus' passion and death, we see that his determination to head toward Jerusalem and to confront the unexamined assumptions of the religious authorities there stems from his discernment of the Father's will and the necessity of proclaiming a new kingdom based on the rule of God's love. His refusal to defend himself, his embrace of the cross, his forgiveness of his executioners, and his final words from the cross stem from the intimate bond he shares with his Father. That bond, which Christians eventually came to call the Holy Spirit, would never be broken, and would later triumph over death and be poured out among his followers at Pentecost.

## LOOKING OUTWARD

In his passion and death, Jesus suffered on every level of his human makeup: the physical, mental, spiritual, and social. As we ponder his pain, we must be careful not to minimalize what he went through by limiting his suffering to mere physical wounds.

The physical torments that Jesus endured are well documented in the Gospel passion narratives.[27] He is spat upon, hit in the face, scourged, crowned with thorns, mocked and scorned, made to carry his cross to the hill outside the city gate, nailed to a cross, and left to die the death of a criminal and outcast. Most of this is done in public, before the very crowd who just days before had hailed him as a prophet as he entered the gates of Jerusalem. So great was the physical pain inflicted upon him that he died after only a few hours of hanging on the cross. In the Roman world, it would often take days for someone to die by crucifixion.

Jesus' mental and emotional anguish appears most visibly in the Gospel accounts of his agony in the Garden of Gethsemane.[28] Although the accounts differ in their details, they together convey an overwhelming sense of someone coming face-to-face with the fear of death and wondering if he will have the strength to bear the physical torments to come. One account even has him falling to the ground and sweating great drops of blood as he asks his heavenly Father if it were possible for this cup of suffering to pass him by.[29] Although he places all of this mental anguish in his Father's hands, its effects reach him to the core and pain him deeply.

Jesus' spiritual anguish is best expressed in his words of desolation from the cross, "My God, my God, why have you forsaken me?"[30] Jesus felt abandoned not only by his closest followers but also by God. In the midst of his intense spiritual anguish, he felt as though he had lost all human and divine support. Alone in his anguish, he might have felt the temptation to despair rise within his heart and reach his lips. Jesus' words of desolation, however, come from the opening verse of Psalm 22, a hymn that begins in inner desolation and torment, but ends in a passionate affirmation of God's ongoing protection and guidance. In alluding to this psalm, Jesus looks beyond his spiritual torment and abandons himself to the love of the Father. At the time of his death, Jesus has nothing to support him but the cross from which he hangs. Despite the downward pull of the earth, he turns his gaze heavenward and gives his tormented spirit over to his Father's care.[31]

Last but not least, Jesus also experienced intense social alienation and humiliation during his passion and death. With few exceptions, the passion narratives correspond closely to what we know of the Roman practice of crucifixion.[32] This form of capital punishment was a common means of execution in Jesus' day and was particularly brutal. It was widespread in ancient times and imposed with special abandon by the Romans on the peoples they subjugated. The purpose of crucifixion was to punish the criminal by means of a slow, painful death—and to set an example so that others would not transgress the law. It took place publicly and in the open air. It began with stripping the criminal and scourging him at the place of judgment. To shame him before the people, he was then forced to carry the cross or crossbeam naked through the streets to the place of execution. Along the way, he was mocked and often spat upon by those who lined the streets. If his strength appeared to be waning, someone was forced to carry the crossbeam for him so that he would not die before he reached the place of execution. The Romans used crucifixion to break down the criminal and portray him as an outcast and enemy of the empire. It was a brutal reminder of Roman occupation and domination. As a Jew, Jesus died a humiliating death on a small hill outside the gates of Jerusalem. The distance away from the holy city was itself a sign of his status as a criminal, a sinner, and an outcast of society.

# Guidelines for Christian Living

The cross is the ultimate expression of God's love for humanity. Contemplating Jesus' passion and death puts us in touch with this love and helps us to recognize God's closeness to us in our own suffering. As Merton puts it, "Jesus did not come to seek God in men. He drew men to Himself by dying for them on the Cross, in order that He might be God in them."[33] Jesus' suffering has much to teach us about the way we should live our lives and face our approaching death. It also has much to show us about the meaning of love and the extent to which we should be willing to express it. However, Jesus does more for us than merely teach and counsel us. His being God in us means that his suffering is now deeply reflected in our own and that he unites ours with his when he offers his suffering to the Father in trustful abandonment. It also means that the story of our life is now intimately related to his and that our own suffering and death must now be viewed in the light of his paschal mystery. The following guidelines give us a glimpse into what Jesus' being God in us means for us.

*We seek to do the will of God in all things.* Jesus sought to do his Father's will in all things. Our intimate communion with Jesus should lead us to do the same. The words of the Our Father teach us to ask that the Father's will be done "on earth as it is in heaven."[34] Allowing God's will to shape what we think, say, and do is really all that matters. God's will for us is that we make his reign of love visible on earth. He has given us his Son as a concrete example of what this means. To do God's will is to follow the way of the Lord Jesus. Like him, we too are called to empty ourselves for others so that they might be free from the burdens that weigh them down and be filled with hope.

*We embrace whatever suffering comes our way when doing God's will.* To build God's reign of love on earth often entails great suffering and hardship. Although relatively few of us will ever be asked to die for Christ, each of us encounters many opportunities each day to die to oneself on behalf of others. In such instances, Christ lives out his passion and death in our long-suffering and patient endurance. We manifest our patience when we put up with the petty annoyances, grievances, and inconveniences of the present moment. Each moment of every day offers us the opportunity to discern God's will for us and embrace it. We are all called to shoulder the cross of the present moment and embrace it as Christ did his own.

*We look upon Jesus' dying words as a testament that he left behind to guide us in times of suffering.* Human societies have often found great solace in the final words of their loved ones. As a person nears his or her final hour and is about to cross the threshold of death, whatever is said is listened to with special reverence and is often considered by those around as a final testament about the meaning of life. By remembering their final words, those we love come closer to us. By pondering their last utterances, we are able to share in their life and death, and their spirits are somehow resurrected in our hearts. Jesus' last utterances from the cross show us how to face suffering and death in the light of faith and a deep trust in God's loving and providential care. By making them our own, we allow Jesus to draw closer to us and live within us.

*We forgive those who harm us.* From the cross Jesus asks his Father to forgive those who were putting him to death.[35] For most of us, forgiving someone who has hurt us is very difficult. It usually involves a long, drawn-out process of claiming the hurt, overcoming guilt for whatever role we might have had in causing it, finally recognizing that we have been victimized, reacting to it in righteous anger, and then moving to wholeness and mutual acceptance.[36] Although not easy to achieve, forgiving becomes less difficult over time. The more we forgive those who have hurt us, the less effort it requires. If we make it a priority in our lives, we gradually find that a deeply rooted attitude has grown within us, one that enables us to face life and all that happens to us with a gentle, forgiving heart. Such an attitude comes not through human effort alone, but in conjunction with God's grace. True forgiveness is a sign of God's presence in our midst. It is a gift from the Lord, one for which all of us should be deeply grateful.

*We yearn for paradise, the peace of God's kingdom.* From the cross, Jesus promises paradise to the good thief dying next to him.[37] When Jesus speaks of paradise, the human heart cannot be far from his thoughts. The good thief was closer to it than he thought. His inner conversion of heart turned him toward Jesus and inspired him to address him. Jesus, in turn, reached out to him in his moment of agony to encourage him and give him hope. Heaven for God was the heart of the good thief. It is every human heart that turns to Jesus and humbly asks him to be born there, grow there, and dwell there. Through Jesus, the distance between the human heart and the heart of God has been bridged. All that remains is for each of us to allow God to walk across the threshold of our hearts and lead us home.

*We look to Mary as our mother.* From the cross, Jesus gives his mother to all of humanity.[38] His death not only brings new meaning to life, but also changes the way we relate to one another. His followers understand the beauty, the power, and the cost of his message of love. They see in the two figures standing at the foot of Jesus' cross a reflection of themselves and the bonds they too wish to forge for the sake of the kingdom. The bond between Mary and the beloved disciple reminds us that the redemption of the world has a great deal to do with changing the way we think and act toward each other. As the mother of Christ's Body, the Church, Mary reminds us of the loving nature of the bonds we are called to share. Because of Jesus, we are all called to be brothers and sisters in faith. In Mary his mother, he provides us, and all members of his family, with a deeply compassionate and caring mother.

*We trust in God in times of desolation.* In his final moments on the cross, Jesus asks God why he has abandoned him.[39] During this time of suffering, he could search for his Father's presence only in the quiet solitude of his heart. He had to suffer the fate of humanity before the Father's response could become evident. Only by dying could the Son of Man be raised. Only by "descending into hell" could he ascend to his rightful place at the Father's right hand. Despite the silence of the Father, he chooses trust over despair in his hour of need. That choice was taken on our behalf and has become for us a legacy of hope. Because of it, we can picture ourselves in his place when we look to the cross. "*Eli, Eli, lama sabachthani?*" become our words; Psalm 22, our prayer; the cross, a sign for us of God's unbroken trust. Jesus suffered the horrors of the cross in order to pass beyond it. The Father raised him on the third day. The day will come when he will do the same for us.

*We thirst for God.* As he hangs from the cross, Jesus says that he is thirsty.[40] His parched throat puts us in touch with the many thirsts of our own human situation. Every dimension of our human makeup gives us something to yearn for. In addition to our bodily wants, we thirst for emotional support, intellectual challenges, human understanding, and spiritual wholeness. We yearn for holiness and wholeness, for health and wellness, for solitude and companionship, for peace and justice. Above all, Jesus' thirst from the cross is a holy thirst. It yearns for the union of the human heart with the divine and of the divine heart with the human. It longs for the coming together of the two and cannot wait until they penetrate each other. Even though he felt abandoned by the Father, Jesus felt this holy thirst intensely. Through his sacrifice on the cross, he imparts this thirst to his followers. Those of us who pick up our crosses and walk in his footsteps experience the same intense yearning for humanity's reconciliation with God.

*We bear suffering that befalls us courageously.* As he hung from the cross, Jesus saw that his work would soon be accomplished.[41] He was relieved to see his end in sight. In his dying moments, he gave himself not only to the Father but also to us. His passion and death stand as a model of courage for his followers to imitate. Down through the centuries, generation upon generation of Christians would look to the cross and see in the bloodied corpus hanging from it both a challenge and a call: The challenge is to dare to trust in Jesus as he trusted in the Father. The call is to pick up our own crosses and follow in his footsteps. Jesus' cross is always calling and challenging us. No matter where we are, it stands as a reminder of someone who gave every ounce of his life for us in order that we might live. His challenge and his call ask us to do the same for others. Jesus' death on the cross seeks to evoke from us a similar response.

*We bring our suffering and needs to God through prayer.* When Jesus commends his spirit to his Father at the moment of death,[42] he offers along with it the spirit of all humanity. In his final act of earthly freedom, he entrusts the human spirit—the vitality and lifeblood of the human race—to the Father's care. This act was something we could not do of our own accord. Someone had to do it for us: someone like us, but also like God; someone human, but also divine. In this final act, Jesus becomes the true mediator between God and man. He takes our place before God and intercedes for us. In his last words, he prays the prayer we longed to but could not pray. He takes us with him as he faces death and places us with him in the Father's care. We face death together, and, because we are in the Father's care, together we shall overcome it. Jesus has identified himself so closely with humanity that his story has become our story, and our story, his. Because of this close identity, we trust that he who suffered and died for us will be there for us in our time of need. Jesus identifies our needs with his needs. Anything we ask the Father in his name, we shall receive.[43]

*We listen to God's Word and, through it, seek to understand God's will for us.* Jesus' obedience flowed from his capacity to listen and understand the Father's will for him. He was able to do so because he shared an intimate relationship with the Father, one that penetrated the core of his being and enabled him to encounter the Father's voice deep within his heart. By becoming man, God's Son united humanity to himself and gave each of us the capacity to hear the Father's voice deep within our hearts. To do so, however, we must empty our hearts of all worldly clutter and turn our inner senses to the subtle movements of God's Spirit. Like Jesus, we too are called to listen for the voice of God within hearts. We too are called to embrace the Father's will for us and follow it out of loving obedience. If we fail to listen to God in the solitude of our hearts, we will never find our true place in the world or understand what God is asking of us.

*We act upon our discernment of God's will for us.* Jesus demonstrated his obedience to the Father through concrete action. He not only listened to and understood the Father's will for him, but also acted upon it. He took the necessary steps to carry it out. Jesus' ministry of preaching and healing was a direct result of his discernment of the Father's will. It was also a prelude to the even greater act of selfless love that he would be asked to make in his passion and death. Jesus not only embraced the Father's will, but also rejoiced in it. He identified himself with it completely, so much so that it was impossible to tell his will from that of his Father's. As his followers and members of his Body, we too are called to act upon our discernment of God's will for us. We must implement what we discern, rejoice in it, and do our best to bring it about.

*We devote ourselves fully to the task God gives us.* Jesus carries out the Father's will with every fiber of his being. Every dimension of his human makeup was involved: the physical, the mental, the spiritual, and the social. He suffered and died not just physically but on every level of his humanity. Every part of him was subject to the claim of death. He understood what was at stake and what was being asked of him. Seeing that everything rested on his shoulders, he embraced his cross knowingly and willingly, with his whole heart, mind, and soul. As his followers and members of his Body, we too are called to give ourselves over fully to God's will for us in our lives. Our following of Christ must not be lukewarm or half-hearted. If we are to identify ourselves as Christians, we need to recognize that our commitment to Jesus should come before all else. We need to dedicate ourselves to him wholeheartedly and without reserve.

*We look beyond our present suffering.* Jesus' trust in the Father's love led him to embrace the cross and look beyond it. He understood that his passion and death were not ends in themselves, but part of a larger providential plan for humanity's redemption. The focus of this plan was the coming of the Father's reign of love on earth through the establishment of a new covenant between God and his people. Jesus, in other words, did not embrace suffering for the sake of suffering, but saw it as a way of reestablishing the lost bond between the divine and human. He suffered and died not because he saw suffering and death as good in themselves, but because he saw his free self-offering as a way of breaking through the hardness of the human heart and enabling it once more to open up to the divine. As followers of Christ and members of his Body, we too are called to look beyond the suffering in our lives and to see it as a participation in that of Christ's. We bear it, even embrace it, because we believe that in Christ it has the power to transform our lives and lead us to something higher.

*We persevere to the end.* Jesus followed the path that his Father had laid out for him until the very end. He did so even when darkness encompassed his path and he could not see clearly ahead. In the midst of the most difficult and trying circumstances, he trusted that his heavenly Father would guide him and bring him to his final destination. Even when he saw that the path before him would lead to the top of Golgotha, he did not flinch from his conviction that he was doing the will of the Father. His determination stems from his love of the Father and his love for humanity. He endured to the end because he did not wish to fail in his love for either. As followers of Christ and members of his Body, we too are called to persevere in life and in our chosen vocations. We are to take up our crosses daily and walk the path that God has laid out for us. In doing so, we walk as true disciples in the footsteps of our Lord and discover with him that the cross opens up a new path leading to our true end, one that begins at the empty tomb and ends at the right hand of the Father.

In the icons of Eastern Christianity, the crucifixion was often depicted as a moment of glory, with the Resurrected Christ nailed to the wood of the cross as a sign of his final triumph over death. Such art reminds us of the cross's power to heal and to transform. It also tells us much about what it means to be a Christian. It teaches us not to fear suffering; it teaches us to look beyond death to something far greater. Through it, we come to see that our relationship with God is something of lasting value and that we must treasure it beyond life itself. Jesus shows us that the fullness of life lies beyond death and that to experience it we must embrace the cross before us and carry it with him to Golgotha. Because of Jesus, the path to death opens up to newness of life in the resurrection. Those of us who believe and follow in his way are called to trust in him as he trusted and gave himself over completely to the will of his Father.

# Conclusion

Jesus' suffering and death are the climax of his process of loving self-emptying, and they offer us many unique insights into the bonds he shares with his Father and with humanity. Although each of these relationships is rooted in divine love, the first manifests itself through filial obedience and the second through fraternal self-sacrifice. The result is a unique and infinite act of self-oblation that reestablishes the broken bond between the human and the divine and "makes holy" the communion between them.

When we contemplate Jesus' suffering and death, we get in touch with our own fragile humanity and find there the mystery of the Father's loving embrace. Because our humanity is now forever one with Christ, his divinity touches and even transforms us through the crucible of his passion and death. Jesus' Seven Last Words become our own. However, we can make them our own only because Jesus has made *us* his own and, in doing so, enabled us to see him as a brother with whom together we cry out, "Abba, Father."[44]

In contemplating Jesus' suffering and death, we have identified a number of guidelines for the Christian life. These spiritual and moral markers spring from our meditative encounter with the events of Golgotha and represent a set of criteria for helping us to determine if we are living the Gospel message authentically. In the hustle and bustle of daily life, such an encounter can come simply by blessing ourselves sincerely and purposefully with the Sign of the Cross. It comes to us in its deepest form, however, by sharing and taking full part in the Church's life and liturgical worship. The goal of these guidelines is to facilitate a movement from contemplation to action so that the attitudes behind Christ's embrace of the cross might become our own and inspire us to follow his lead.

## CONTEMPLATING THE FACE OF CHRIST

1. Do you believe that there was "a cross in God before the wood was seen on Calvary"?[45] What do you mean by it? Is there more than one way to understand this statement? What does this statement say about God's nature? What does it say about the relationship between love and suffering? Can God suffer and yet also be beyond suffering?

2. Do Jesus' Seven Last Words speak to you? If so, on what level? Do they speak to you personally? How are you moved by them? What message are they

trying to communicate? Which of them touches you most deeply? Which of them touches you the least? Do you view these words as a kind of testament? How should Christians respond to them?

3. What is the relationship between obeying, listening, and understanding? How do they interact? Is it possible to obey without having the capacity to listen? Is it possible to obey without having the capacity to understand? Why is obedience such an important Christian virtue? Is there a difference between true and false obedience? To what extend is obedience oriented toward action?

4. What are your attitudes toward suffering and death? Does your head tell you one thing and your heart another? Do you react to them in different ways at different times? How would you like to be able to react to them? What do you need to do to get you to that point? Does Jesus' embrace of his own suffering and death help you in any way?

## FOLLOWING THE PROMPTINGS OF THE SPIRIT

Make a list of your present hardships and difficulties. In what areas of your life do you suffer the most: physical illness, material hardship, psychological distress, mental handicap, social inadequacy, spiritual torment? Try to be as specific as possible by identifying not only the area of pain in your life, but also its specific characteristics. What sickness do you have? What are your material needs? What are you most anxious about? What challenges you intellectually? What difficulties do you have relating socially? Why do you feel alone and spiritually isolated? After you have made your list as specific as possible, try to imagine the sufferings of Jesus as he undergoes his passion and death. Try to feel his pain as he utters his Seven Last Words from the cross. Listen not only to his words, but also to his spirit, soul, and heart. Ponder the crucifix or imagine Jesus' bloodied corpus in your mind. Watch him as he commends his spirit to his Father and breathes his last. Now pray to Jesus. Bless yourself with the Sign of the Cross. Recognize that Jesus has taken all of your sufferings and the sufferings of those you love, and, indeed, the sufferings of all of humanity, upon himself. Understand that your list of sufferings is now Jesus'. All you need to do is give them to him by releasing your heart into his, thus making the cross he carries and hangs from your own.

# CHAPTER SIX

# Contemplating Jesus' Resurrection

In the theology of redemption, the point of departure for reflection is not sin needing to be repaired, nor is it Christ's death as a means to satisfy God's offended justice. Christian faith was born in the encounter with the risen One; likewise, theological reflection takes its point of departure from the risen One. He who is the Omega is also the Alpha. The Resurrection is the work of the Father who begets-creates the Son into the world for its salvation. The Resurrection is the summit and the symbol of all the Father's activity—that Father who is the origin of everything. Theology can only understand the death of Jesus in the light of the Resurrection.

F. X. Durrwell, *Christ Our Passover*[1]

Have you ever thought of the resurrection as an impossible idea, as one almost too good to be true? I know I have. For years I considered it beyond the realm of possibility, as something that sounded nice, but did not have any real teeth to it. It was an entertaining thought, but not much else. It did not seem grounded in reality, at least the reality I knew. It might be attractive to the quixotic types who loved to chase windmills and rescue would-be damsels, but I knew better: *my* two feet were planted firmly on the ground. I believed in God, but it seemed to me that there were some things that even God would not (or could not) do—and raising people from the dead was one of them.

---

In this final chapter, we will contemplate the role played by Jesus' resurrection in humanity's redemption and look at its plausibility both as an idea and a belief. We will ponder the possibility of it happening and, if so, why it happened and what it means and symbolizes. We will also ask some difficult questions regarding its relevance for the world today. Our goal here will be to see what the Risen One has to say to us about our present situation and destiny. As F. X. Durrwell asserts, "The Resurrection is the final stage, and it will be for the Church. The history of Jesus and the Church was accomplished in the Resurrection. However, everything begins there for Jesus and the Church, as well."[2] Jesus can claim to be "the Alpha and the Omega, the first and the last, the beginning and the end"[3] because of his relationship to the Father and what the Father has accomplished in him.

## The Resurrection of Jesus

At the very outset, it is important for us to recognize that the Christian doctrine of the resurrection goes beyond our wildest hopes and deepest imaginings. It seems to have more in common with myth and fairy tale than with the realities of human history. Its premise seems too improbable, too far-fetched, too much of an unrealizable ideal for it to be true or to have any concrete relevance for our lives. Am I not right?

Perhaps, perhaps not. Few things in life lie completely beyond the realm of doubt, even belief in the resurrection. Human experience teaches us that what is most noble and true about our lives often lies far beyond our grasp. For example, the whole point of Cervantes' classic novel *Don Quixote* (1615) is to make us examine some of our most basic assumptions about what is real and unreal, true and false, sane and insane. As the erstwhile knight roams the Spanish countryside striving to keep his ideal of chivalry alive, he encounters one adventurous mishap after another and near the end of the novel reaches the state of near-disillusionment himself. He changes people's hearts in the process, however, and enables them to see the world in an entirely different way, with eyes they never had before.

The truth of the resurrection should not be discounted merely because of its strange, seemingly unlikely character. The Apostle Paul traveled the Roman world because he was knocked off his horse and seized by a vision more real than any dream.[4] Like him, we must "walk by faith, not by sight."[5] If we do, we will see things we never saw before and experience life in an entirely different way. The idea of resurrection would be one of them. If God truly exists and loves humanity the way the Christian faith says he does, it follows that he would devise a form of afterlife uniquely fitting for those he created in his own image and likeness. If there is a gap between our present human reality and the idea of the resurrection, our faith tells us that it can be bridged by God, for whom all things are possible.[6] He alone can make this seemingly impossible dream come true.

What can we say about the resurrection, first as an idea and then as a reality? Rooted in the hopes of Jewish apocalypticism in the centuries just prior to Jesus' birth, and promulgated during his lifetime by the devout religious group known as the Pharisees, the idea of resurrection developed to its present form as a result of theological reflection on the nature of the Christ event, most especially in the primitive Christian community's interpretation of the meaning of the apostolic experience of the Risen Lord.[7] This reflection is intimately related both to the trust that the community placed in the validity of the apostolic witness and to the experience of faith upon which it rested. It is also the context within which we may speak of the resurrection not as an idea, but as a reality and a hope.

What precisely happened on that first Easter morning remains shrouded by the eschatological character of the event itself and by the subjective awareness of the earliest followers of

Jesus. That awareness probably ran the gamut of several emotional states and most likely varied in each of the persons involved. That is not to say that the event has no basis outside the experience of Jesus' followers, but only that we cannot determine what it is with any historical accuracy. The Easter event, in other words, touches history, but extends far beyond it. Probably the most important consequence of this unique eschatological/historical encounter is the faith experience of Jesus' immediate followers that provided the original impetus for the rise and spread of the earliest Christian communities.[8] The faith of the Church universal rests upon the foundation of these earliest apostolic witnesses.

At this point, we must make an important distinction between the faith of those who witnessed the Easter event personally and those whose faith relies on the testimony of the apostles. The proclamation of the Church rests upon the eyewitness accounts of the apostles; that is, upon those who made the startling claim to have experienced for themselves the reality of the Risen Lord. Their experience of faith remains qualitatively different from that of other believers, for they claim to have experienced a reality outside of themselves, rooted in the objective order, distinct from their own subjectivity, and identified with the person of their Master, Jesus of Nazareth. Without the unprecedented boldness and resiliency of these claims, Christianity would have nothing distinctive in its message and possibly might never have survived.[9]

These apostolic claims emerge from one of two possibilities: the experience of the risen Christ was *with* or *without* a basis in the person of Jesus in the external order. In other words, the experience of the apostles corresponds to a reality outside themselves or remains entirely subjective in all respects. If the former is true, then we must ask a further question regarding the nature of this basis in the external order. If the latter is true, then the only conclusion to be drawn is that the apostles suffered from self-delusion, that their testimony is false, as is the religion to which it gave rise. The fact that we cannot prove either of these possibilities highlights the underlying quality of faith inherent in the conclusions of both the believer and nonbeliever alike.

We can say still more about the position of the believer. If the apostolic experience of the risen Christ *does* have an external basis in the person of Jesus, then this affirmation necessarily points to an event of singular historical significance, indeed, an event that could be measured by the instruments of historical observation only by its effects (for example, a missing body) and that, for this reason, must be placed in a category unique to itself and understood as a transhistorical event with historical consequences. We say this because the risen Christ, existing in a transformed state but in a way continuous with his earthly life, does not lead "a historical existence" in the way in which the phrase is commonly used. That is to say that space and time no longer set the limits for his physical existence. In his resurrected state, Christ is the Alpha and the Omega, a singular dimension unique unto himself, who now and forever recapitulates all of creation in himself into the love of the Father and the joy of their Spirit.[10]

# Contemplating Jesus' Resurrection

What does this mean for us concretely? How do these insights about Jesus' resurrection affect our daily lives? Deep down inside, everyone needs a dream to live by. Whenever we profess our faith, we proclaim that Jesus rose from the dead and thus we make his dream our own. We make this assertion based on the experience of many of his closest followers and their insistence that he had appeared to them after his death in a transformed bodily state. By making this claim, we assert what many believe to be impossible—that in Jesus of Nazareth the process of death was somehow reversed. What is more, we claim not only that his body and soul were reunited, but also that he was elevated ("lifted up," if you will) to a new level of existence. This transformation was accomplished by the Father in the Son for the good of humanity and has important repercussions for our spiritual moral lives.

Death: our deepest fear and oldest foe! What could be more practical, more promising, and more meaningful for our everyday lives than to overcome it? Thomas Merton puts it this way: "The sanctity of Christian life is based not on love of an abstract law but on love of the living God, a divine person, Jesus Christ, the Incarnate Word of God, who has redeemed us and delivered us from the darkness of sin and death."[11] In keeping with the approach we have taken in this book, we will now try to show how contemplating Jesus' resurrection can have a direct impact on our lives as Christians. We will examine this seemingly "Impossible Dream" and see what it means for us in the warp and woof of our daily lives.

## LOOKING INWARD

To begin with, Jesus' resurrection has its roots in the intimate communion between the Father and the Son. As such, it has an eternal dimension to it, one that goes beyond the limited dimensions of space and time of that first Easter morning. The resurrection, we can say, existed in God before the stone was rolled back from the tomb.

As we contemplate Jesus' resurrection, it is important for us to recognize its roots in the mutual love between the Father and the Son. If the cross is the Son's loving response to the Father's will, then the resurrection is the Father's manifestation of his unconditional love for the Son. The love that binds them is manifested in Jesus' paschal mystery and poured out upon the world at Pentecost through the Holy Spirit. When seen in this light, the resurrection is intimately related to the cross—and vice versa. While the cross is the Son's response to the Father's will, the resurrection is the Father's response to the Son's obedient acceptance of the cross. Each, in turn, is a direct expression of the Spirit that binds them and through which they share an intimate communion.

Since the resurrection is intimately related to the cross and is present in the very heart of God from all eternity, it has a timeless dimension that conveys something special about divine love. "God is love,"[12] we are told, and that love is transformative by its very nature. It is constantly going beyond itself and changing both itself and everything it touches. The fathers of the Church expressed this very well when they described love as being "self-diffusive."[13] God's love, while eminently free, cannot contain itself and is naturally oriented toward the other. While the doctrine of the Trinity expresses this truth within the Godhead, the doctrines of creation, redemption, and sanctification do so for God's outward activity, which flows from his being and seeks to order all of reality to it.

The transforming nature of divine love gives us a dynamic sense of God's very being, which, at the same time, is both one and three. When seen in this light, unity and multiplicity find their resolution in the metaphysical juxtaposition of Being and Relation in the mystery of God's eternal Love. Father, Son, and Spirit are distinct from one another by virtue of their differences in relationship, making the Godhead relational in its very essence.[14] But since Essence and Being are the same in God, the opposite conclusion is also true: the Divinity is distinct by virtue of its oneness of being and one by virtue of its distinctive relationships.

When contemplating Jesus' resurrection as an expression of the transforming power of divine love, we begin to see it in an entirely different light. If, as we said earlier, the cross is a sign of the Son's love for the Father, and the resurrection one of the Father's love for the Son, then together they represent a concrete representation of the love that binds them. The bond of love within the Godhead lies in the timeless kenotic self-emptying of the Son and the eternally elevating and transforming response of the Father. Christ's paschal mystery thus lies in the very heart of God and is intimately related to the Holy Spirit, in whose love we are baptized and incorporated into Christ as members of his Body, the Church. In our practical daily lives, we must never overlook this intrinsic connection between Jesus' cross and his resurrection from the dead. The risen Christ, we are told, still bears the wounds of his passion and death.[15] The same holds true for us. As members of his Body, our own wounds and brokenness—whatever they are and wherever they may be—are intimately related to his.[16]

## LOOKING OUTWARD FROM WITHIN

As we continue to ponder Jesus' resurrection, our gaze shifts from the intimate bond shared by the Father and the Son from all eternity, to the Father's gripping and engaging stare at the lifeless body of his Son after he was taken down from the cross and laid in the tomb. The Father contemplates his Son, not only from all eternity, but even as the Son enters our world and lays down his life for us. The Father ponders his Son as the Word Incarnate, who enters human experience to reveal the mysteries of divine love.[17]

This love manifests itself in the passion and death of Jesus, which reverberates not only throughout creation, but also within the heavens. This event shakes humanity to the core and evokes an outpouring of the Father's compassion upon the cosmos. Jesus gave up his life out of love for humanity and followed the will of the Father to the very end. As the Father ponders this sacrificial self-offering, the love he bears for his Son proves even mightier than death. The results are startling and seem nearly beyond belief. Death has been overwhelmed by the power of the Spirit. The terrors of the cross cannot break the bond between the Father and the Son. Mortality makes its claim on Jesus' humanity, but is overcome by the Father's transforming love.

The resurrection is about the reversal of the process of death and humanity's final transformation in the person of Jesus Christ. This reversal comes about through the power of divine love; more specifically, through the Father's compassionate love for his divine-and-human Son who willingly accepts his death. The transformation entails a divinization of Jesus' humanity, made possible by the Father through his intimate relationship with the Son. Because of the incarnation, Jesus' relationship with the Father extends not only to his divinity, but also to his humanity. Because of the resurrection, Jesus' humanity has become divinized (i.e., permeated by the divine and elevated to a higher level of existence) and offered to us as a means of sharing in the love of the Father for the Son. Our participation in Jesus' humanity comes about through the waters of baptism and our sharing in his paschal mystery.[18]

The miracle of the resurrection celebrates the love of the Father for his Son and for all of humanity. Because of the resurrection, we enjoy the privilege of being the Father's adopted sons and daughters and have the hope of sitting with Jesus at the right hand of the Father. When the Father gazes upon the lifeless corpse of his Son, he ponders also the reason behind his Son's making himself one with the weakness of human flesh. The Son took on our humanity in order to heal us of our wounds and to bridge the distance between the human and the divine. When the Father raises the Son on the third day, those wounds are closed and the distance between God and humanity traversed. Our humanity is lifted up with the Son's. The Father's compassionate, transforming love flows into Jesus' humanity and, through it, to our own. The end result is more than we could ever possibly have imagined.[19]

## LOOKING INWARD FROM WITHOUT

As we continue our contemplation of the resurrection, we turn to the actual moment when Jesus entered this world a second time, not by being born from a mother's womb, but by being raised to new life. At that instant, Jesus' body, soul, and spirit—his humanity—were reunited and elevated to a transformed level of existence. Jesus' humanity, which exists in a distinctly personal union with his divinity (i.e., in a hypostatic union), is now itself completely divinized. In this transformed state, Jesus becomes the New Adam, the firstborn of the new creation who draws all of humanity, and indeed the entire cosmos, to himself.[20]

As we ponder Jesus in this newly transformed state, we imagine him opening his eyes and marveling at the work the Father has wrought in him. Raised from the dead, he experiences his body anew, as if for the first time. His physical presence is the same, yet strangely different, for he is able to do things never before possible. His body is physical, yet no longer limited by the dimensions of time and space. He can appear as if out of nowhere, and yet can eat and drink as in his former state. He senses the world around him in a much deeper way. The taste, touch, sound, sight, and smell of things seems fuller and more complete than before. The same is true for his internal senses of memory and imagination, which also have been transformed and which allow him to experience his past and imagine his future in ways beyond his deepest dreams. Even his human spirit seems connected to God in new and exciting ways as new dimensions of his humanity open up to receive more of the Father's unconditional love.

In his risen state, Jesus senses that he has passed through a terrible ordeal and, looking down at the holes of his wounded hands, recalls all of its myriad and gruesome details. The marks of his passion imprinted in his body remind him of the suffering he has undergone. All the physical, psychological, and spiritual pain comes back to him, and he experiences it now in a different way. Although suffering and death have touched the very core of his being, he sees that even they could not withstand the power of the Father's love for his trusting and obedient Son. They have been defeated and no longer have the final say in the fragile narrative of human life. As his wounds remind us, Jesus does not leave suffering and death behind, but brings them with him as he enters his resurrected state. He does so that we might find meaning in our own suffering and learn to live in hope.

Jesus lets out a breath and senses the Spirit within him as he looks back on what has occurred with a deep sense of gratitude to the Father for all the marvels he has wrought. A new heaven and a new earth have now come into existence. God has become human; humanity, divinized. Suffering and death have been overcome. The cross has given way to an empty tomb, and Jesus is about to appear to his disciples. Jesus sees the wonder of all this and turns to his Father in praise and thanksgiving. His Father did not abandon him in his time of need, but rescued him from the jaws of death and raised him to new life for his own good and for the good of all humanity. Jesus' gratitude to the Father would soon overflow into the hearts of his closest disciples and the Easter proclamation would joyfully resound from their lips—and from ours, as well.[21]

## LOOKING OUTWARD

"The Lord has risen indeed, and he has appeared to Simon!"[22] These words of the apostles place Jesus' resurrection at the very heart of the Easter proclamation. As we continue to ponder the Risen Lord, our gaze turns now toward his appearances to his disciples and to the message that he gave them.

Once Jesus has pondered the nature and scope of his transformed existence, it would be natural for him to enter the world and show himself to those who loved him. Although he did not need to roll back the stone (since he could have moved right through it in his elevated state), he does so to draw attention to what has occurred and to send a message to the world that something strange indeed has happened in the aftermath of the death of Jesus of Nazareth. The accounts of Jesus' appearances show that, although he was not easily recognized, he was not considered a ghost or a phantom, but someone with very physical dimensions who could speak with his disciples, build a fire, reveal his wounds, and even eat. At the same time, it was also clear to them that he could move through closed doors and move about freely through space and time. Furthermore, he appeared not only to small intimate gatherings of his followers, but to large groups. In the case of Paul, moreover, he appeared a number of years after his earlier appearances to his disciples.[23]

Just as important as Jesus' appearances to his disciples was the message he imparted to them. There were three main dimensions of this message: to be without fear, to be at peace, and to proclaim his message. Sometimes, the message not to fear is conveyed by an angel; at other times, it comes directly from Jesus himself. The purpose of this aspect of his message is to calm whatever fears the disciples might have regarding their relationship to their Lord. Jesus, in other words, has risen from the dead not to cause harm or to instill fear, but to bring to the world the peace that he shares by virtue of his intimate communion with the Father. Because of this communion, the disciples have nothing to fear from Jesus or from the world. Jesus imparts his peace to his disciples in a number of resurrection accounts. This peace possesses both inner and outer dimensions. Interiorly, Jesus is sharing with his disciples the deep sense of tranquility that his paschal mystery has brought him. He shares with them a peace that the world cannot give, something that comes from his trusting obedience to the Father as manifested in his embrace of the cross and the Father's transforming love expressed in Jesus' resurrection.

Outwardly, Jesus encourages his disciples to share this peace with others. This takes place by forgiving others and also in proclaiming his message to the world. This third element of his message to his disciples—that of proclamation—appears in all four Gospel accounts, as well as in the Acts of the Apostles.

Jesus' commission to his disciples to proclaim the Good News to the ends of the earth flows directly from their experience of the Risen Lord. They believed in the continuity between the earthly and resurrected Jesus and saw their proclamation of the Gospel as a continuation of Jesus' public ministry.

Jesus affirmed this continuity through the gift of his Spirit, whom he poured out upon the gathering of his disciples at Pentecost, an event that made each believer a member of his Body, the Church. The gift of the Spirit to the Church confirms each dimension of Jesus' post-resurrection message. Because of the Spirit, Jesus' disciples know that he is always with them and that there is nothing to fear. Because of the Spirit, they also experience the peace of Christ, which comes to them through the mediation of the Church in its celebration of Word and Sacrament. Because of the Spirit, they have the courage to proclaim Jesus' message in their daily lives through both word and deed. The same holds true for us today. Because of the Spirit, our impossible dream has become a tangible, concrete reality in our lives.[24]

# Guidelines for Christian Living

Proclaiming the reality of the Risen Lord remains the primary message of Jesus' Body, the Church. As Durrwell puts it, "Everything began when Jesus rose. 'He is risen!' was the cry of the Church at its birth. Faith was stirred up on the day of Easter in the encounter with the risen One. In our own days it is still set on fire through that encounter."[25] As the following guidelines demonstrate, Jesus' resurrection has much to tell us about the way we should live our lives and the message we should always seek to convey through our thoughts, words, and deeds.

*We embrace death as a part of life.* Jesus' resurrection must be interpreted in the light of his passion and death—and vice versa. As the Father contemplated the loving self-offering of his

Son, he was moved by the extent to which he was willing to go to express his love for humanity. Jesus gave himself completely, to the point of dying for us. Although he did not see death as a good in itself, he understood that it had become an integral part of the human story and that by becoming one of us, he too had to undergo the painful and heartrending separation of body and soul. Jesus embraced the cross in solidarity with the whole human family. By becoming one of us, he steered humanity in a new direction and led us to our home in the heart of God. As his followers, we too embrace death as a part of life and place ourselves entirely in the loving hands of the Father.

*We look beyond the present world.* Jesus' resurrection gives us a new way of looking at life and death. It helps us look beyond the present world to one that is still to come and yet, in some sense, is already in our midst. It does so by telling us that life in the present world is a preparation for another still to come, one that exceeds our greatest hopes and desires. By promising us communion with God, fellowship with one another, and fullness of life, Jesus' resurrection helps us live in the present with renewed strength and heightened expectations. It challenges us to look beyond the present world: not to escape it, but to engage it more fully and so be instruments of the world's transformation. It signals the dawn of the new creation, one where death has no claim over us and where life itself has been lifted to new heights.

*We believe in miracles.* Jesus' resurrection from the dead occurred both in and out of time. To accept it as something more than a mere subjective experience, to accept it as an event that actually took place in the external order, forces us to examine many of the underlying assumptions of our present worldview. To believe in the resurrection is to affirm, not only the reality of God's existence, but also his intervention in the world he has created. While the resurrection is the only miracle necessary to the Christian worldview, to accept it means that we recognize God's power to suspend the laws of nature and act in the world directly. The resurrection recognizes God as the Lord of creation, the Lord of history, and the Lord of time and space.

*We seek to foster intimacy in our relationships.* It has been said that intimacy involves two primary elements: self-disclosure and loving attention.[26] For Christians, the reciprocal love between the Father and the Son is the most intimate relationship of all. The Father discloses his will to the Son, who listens and lovingly follows. The Father, in turn, responds to the Son's incarnation, life, suffering, and death by raising him from the dead on Easter morning. Both Father and Son are forever disclosing themselves to one another and forever responding with loving attention. The eternal bond between them that we have come to know as the Holy Spirit was poured out on the Church at Pentecost and moves us to bring God's love to others. That love comes from and leads to intimacy. Whenever we foster authentic relationships based on mutual self-disclosure and loving attention, we make God's reign of love present on earth and in the human heart.

*We trust the testimony of the apostles.* A basic difference exists between those who personally experienced Jesus on that first Easter morning and those whose faith depends on this early apostolic witness. We maintain that the testimony of the Church rests on the eyewitness testimony of Jesus' closest and most intimate followers. The apostles claimed to have seen the Risen Lord, the person to whom they had dedicated their lives and whom they loved beyond all telling. This experience was not a figment of their imagination or a psychological projection, but something rooted in the external, objective order. They proclaimed that Jesus of Nazareth, who was crucified by the Romans, had risen from the dead and continued to live in a transformed, glorified state. They kept this insight alive in the primitive Christian community and made it the heart of their Gospel proclamation. This belief in the objective reality of Jesus' resurrection is the very source of the Christian faith. It continues to shape our outlook on the meaning of life, as well as the way we interpret past, present, and future.

*We believe that Love is stronger than death.* Jesus' resurrection was an act of the Father's love for his only begotten Son. To believe that it is not merely an idea or a myth or a subjective experience, but that it actually occurred, says something about our understanding of the power of love and its ability to overcome evil. Jesus' resurrection announces the inability of death to overcome God's love for humanity. It affirms Love as the ultimate ground of reality and claims that it has unleashed its power on the world to turn back the forces of nature and bring back to life someone who had succumbed to the power of death and decay. Belief in the resurrection not only enables us to live in the hope that our deepest human potential will one day be fully actualized, but also encourages us to instill that hope in others.

*We live in hope.* If divine experience became humanized in the incarnation, then the reverse took place on Easter Sunday morning. In Jesus' resurrection, human experience became divinized. On that day, our humanity ("human nature," if you will) was lifted up by God, healed, elevated, and brought into his presence. As a result, we can now listen for the voice of God in the circumstances of our daily lives and live in the hope that one day we too shall share in the fullness of God's life. This hope gives us the courage to face the hardships of daily life and to listen for the voice of God in all that happens to us. Jesus lived in the hope that God's love would reign in our hearts and forever banish hatred from world. His resurrection reveals to us the power of God's love and shows us something of our destiny as God's adopted sons and daughters.

*We believe that the idea of resurrection became a reality in the person of Jesus.* The notion of resurrection involves belief in a personal life after death, in a transformed state that embraces all the anthropological dimensions of human existence in a way continuous with an individual's concrete, earthly life. As

Christians, we believe that the resurrection is not a mere intellectual idea, but is an actual reality that took place some three days after Jesus' death on the cross. This event lies at the very heart of the Christian proclamation and says something very significant about humanity's destiny. We believe that our lives are now intertwined with Christ's and that the story of our lives is now a part of his paschal mystery. Because of Jesus' resurrection, we believe that we too shall be raised to new life and enter into the presence of the Father.

*We believe that Jesus' resurrection marks the beginning of a new creation, and we yearn for its coming.* Jesus' resurrection was not only a salvific but also an eschatological event. It initiated God's redemptive plan for humanity and points to its fulfillment at the end of time. It is an already-but-not-yet reality revealing the power of God's love to the world, yet awaiting its full and final manifestation. Jesus' rising to new life marks the beginning of God's renewal of the created order. Through it, God has reclaimed a world gone awry through the evil wrought by cosmic and human forces. Through the Spirit of the Resurrected Lord, he lifts the world to new heights as he reshapes it into something new, into something even better than it was before. This same Spirit yearns in our hearts as we await this new creation and herald its coming.

*We believe that through baptism we are incorporated into Christ's paschal mystery and become members of his Body.* Jesus' resurrection was not only a personal but also a communal event. It happened not only to Jesus, but also to everyone who is baptized into his paschal mystery and confesses him as Lord and Savior. Since Jesus' humanity is also our own, he took us with him in his passion and death and in his new life when the Father raised him. His transformed humanity forms the basis of his Mystical Body, the Church, and extends to all who are baptized into that Body as members. We share in Jesus' resurrection through our participation in the Church's life and mission. As such, we have become Jesus' eyes and ears in the world today and seek to do everything possible to foster his rule of love in ourselves and others.

*We live without fear.* When he appeared to them after his resurrection, Jesus told his disciples not to be afraid. With the risen Lord at our side, there is nothing to fear and no cause for anxiety. Jesus has passed through death and risen to new life. He has embraced our humanity and transformed it. Because of him, no real harm can come to it. Someone once said that the motto of false religion is: "Fear not; trust in God and he will see that none of the things you fear will happen to you." The motto of true religion, on the contrary, is: "Fear not; the things that you are afraid of are quite likely to happen to you, but they are nothing to be afraid of."[27] Christianity is true religion at its best. It relativizes suffering by affirming the power of the risen Lord and reminding us that perfect love drives out all fear.[28]

*We live in peace and seek to promote it.* When he appeared to his disciples after his resurrection, Jesus greeted them in peace and promised that he would send them his Spirit. This peace comes from his intimate communion with his Father. It comes as a gift freely given and must be received and welcomed as such. It is impossible to force someone to be at peace against his or her will. Jesus' peace comes to us as "peace of heart," an inner sense of tranquility and well-being that rests in our hearts through the work of the Spirit. It is nurtured in us through prayer, fasting, and almsgiving, and especially through our sharing in the life of the Church. Jesus' peace has consequences for the way we live our lives. If we are truly at peace with God and ourselves, then we will seek to communicate that peace with others. We do so by treating others with respect and by doing our best to promote a just and lasting peace on the various levels of human society.

*We proclaim to all the world the Good News of life in the risen Christ.* After his resurrection, Jesus commissioned his disciples to preach the Good News to all the earth. The heart of this proclamation is the apostolic experience of the Risen Lord and the new life that we hope to share as a result of it. We are able to proclaim this message because of the peace we experience in our hearts and the belief that the Risen Lord is with us as we work for the coming of his kingdom. We proclaim this message on many levels (among family and friends, in the parish and local community, on the national and world stages) and in many ways (by example and explicit proclamation, through educational and charitable institutions, by efforts for peace and social justice). We do so to be faithful to our call to discipleship and to make God's love visible to the world today.

*We believe that, although the Risen Lord has returned to the Father, he is still with us and will remain so forever.* Jesus has commissioned us to carry his message to the ends of the earth, but he has not given us this task to carry out all alone. He has made us members of his Body and has also given us his Spirit to carry on his work of preaching, healing, and sanctifying. As such, he is not only present to us, but also lives in us and works through us. Jesus' promise to be with us has great significance for the Christian spiritual moral life. The company we keep can have a great impact on the way we live our lives. As Christians, we seek to keep company with the Lord so that our thoughts and attitudes, as well as our words and actions, might be like his. We do this especially through prayer, which has been described as nothing else than "keeping company with God."[29]

*We believe that we receive a foretaste of the resurrection whenever we celebrate at the table of the Lord.* At Emmaus, Jesus' disciples recognized him in the breaking of the bread.[30] We seek the same when we gather in churches throughout the world to celebrate the Eucharist. The sacraments are actions of the risen Christ in the members of his Body, the Church. When we gather for Eucharist, Jesus is present to the body of believers who have gathered for worship. As head of his Body, he offers praise, glory, and thanksgiving to the Father in the Spirit. The Eucharist immerses us in the one sacrifice of Calvary, gives us the Body and

Blood of the Risen Lord to eat when we receive communion, and gives us a foretaste of the heavenly banquet. As such, it is the summit of the Christian life, our ongoing point of contact with the Risen Lord, and the source from which we receive the nourishment we need for leading the Christian spiritual moral life.

Jesus' resurrection has much to tell us about the Christian spiritual moral life. It reminds us of our destiny in God and that Jesus is the way to get there. It also reminds us that our actions in this life are meant to flow from our intimate contact with Jesus, the Risen Lord, who has entrusted us with the task of spreading his message of God's love for the world and who promises to be with us as we carry out this task. The spiritual moral life of Christians is a vital part of this task. Jesus' message is spread primarily through the witness of saintly lives, of people who are thoroughly committed to following their Lord. Their lives are an expression of Jesus' Spirit who dwells within their hearts and leads them to proclaim, with the earliest witnesses of the Easter faith, "He is risen!"

## Conclusion

What can we say by way of conclusion? In the first place, Jesus' resurrection is nothing less than an impossible dream come true, one that keeps alive in us the hope that our lives will continue after death. Because of Easter morning, we look forward to a transformed existence in the hereafter, one in continuity with our own lives on earth and rooted in our faith in the Risen Lord. Sustained by our prayerful response to the contemporary challenges of Christian discipleship, this hope forms the basis upon which life in the resurrection is anticipated even in the present.

Second, although we affirm that Jesus' resurrection has a ground in the external order, we recognize that it lies beyond the pale of empirical observation. For this reason, the faith of those who experienced the Risen Lord is qualitatively different from those of us whose faith rests upon their testimony. We believe without seeing and thus share in the hope of our own transformed existence kept alive through our experience of the Spirit in the community of the faithful. We also believe that this future existence may be experienced even now in quiet anticipation of the fullness of a reality yet to come. This happens especially when we bring our hearts' deepest yearning for the fullest presence of the risen Christ to the table of the Lord, where we are blessed with a glimpse of his continuing presence in our eucharistic breaking of the bread.

Finally, as Christians we believe that Jesus, the Risen Lord, is the Alpha and Omega, the Beginning and the End, who recapitulates all of creation in himself and carries it into the love of the Father and the joy of the Spirit. By centering our lives entirely on him, we seek to live in his Spirit in a way that anticipates the fullness of the transformation of all things in the life to come. By living in this way, we serve as a leaven for both ourselves and others seeking the presence of the Lord in their midst and make good on Christ's promise to remain with us always, even until the end of time.

## CONTEMPLATING THE FACE OF CHRIST

1. How would you respond to those who say that Christianity is mainly about the message of love taught by Jesus and not about his resurrection from the dead? What does belief in Jesus' resurrection bring to the Christian faith? How are his messages of love and resurrection related? Can they be separated without doing damage to the Christian proclamation? Why do so many people have a hard time believing in Jesus' resurrection?

2. Do you believe in miracles? What is required for one to take place? How does one occur and why?

What prevents someone from believing in miracles? Is faith required for miracles to occur? Is it required for recognizing one when it *has* occurred? Do you believe in the miracle of Jesus' resurrection? Do you believe that this miracle will one day also happen to you?

3. Do you think that the experience of the Risen Lord of the apostles and other close disciples of Jesus was a purely subjective experience or did it have some basis in the external order? Do you think that this distinction between subjective experience and the external order is valid? If not, why not? How is your faith in the Risen Lord different from that of the apostles? How is it similar?

4. How did the experience of the Risen Lord change the lives of the apostles? What new insights did it give them? How did it embolden them? Where did they find the courage to proclaim the Easter message? What is the relationship between their experience of the Risen Lord and the gift of the Spirit? Do you think you have experienced the Risen Lord? Do you think you have experienced his Spirit? If so, in what way has this experience changed your life?

## FOLLOWING THE PROMPTINGS OF THE SPIRIT

"Grace," we are told, "builds on nature." If this is so, then it follows that there are vestiges or traces of the resurrection present in the world around us. People point to the transformation of a caterpillar and how, after spinning its cocoon and lying dormant all during the winter months, it turns into a butterfly with the arrival of spring. Various other forms of hibernation, even sleep itself, point to a natural cycle in all living organisms that moves from death-like stillness to newness of life. Jesus himself gives an example from nature: "Unless a grain of wheat falls into the earth and dies, it remains just a single grain; but if it dies, it bears much fruit."[31]

What vestiges of the resurrection do you see in the world around you? Do you believe that they are signs of what is yet to come? Do you see any in your own life? What are your impossible dreams? In what ways is grace building on *your* nature? How do you see God working in your life and quietly changing you in the person he wishes you to become?

# A Manifesto for Contemplative Ethics

At the end of our discussion, we can now offer the following manifesto for our new discipline and field of inquiry.

Contemplative ethics requires a continuous backdrop of inner silence or solitude of heart. It bids us to consider every dimension of our human makeup in the light of Jesus Christ, the New Man. It embraces a threefold movement of contemplation, communion, and mission. It focuses not only on human actions and the virtues needed to perform them, but also on the attitudes we must have to sustain the options we have chosen to direct us. It encourages serious reflection on particular issues and the decisions to be made concerning them. It involves naming and taking ownership of our feelings about areas of moral concern. It requires identifying the personal and social needs involved in our decisions. It bids us to look to the area of concrete action.

Contemplative ethics requires that we search out stillness. When practicing contemplative ethics, we engage in active listening. We recognize and accept our place in the universe. We value and form right relationships. We act as mediators. We foster communion at various levels. We ponder our situation from afar. We seek to heal and transform. We live in the service of others. We empathize with others and are involved in their lives. We act out of love for others.

We are committed to building up the kingdom. We recognize the uniqueness of our actions. We seek the infinite in the bounds of the finite. We bring our actions to prayer.

When practicing contemplative ethics, we have a deep respect for creation and the material world. We cultivate a sense of wonder about the world around us. We strive to integrate the contemplative and action-oriented dimensions of our lives. We use appropriate and fitting means to achieve our intended goals. We foster a respect for the human person. We contemplate and deeply respect the various stages of human life. We recognize the various levels of human sinfulness. We seek to enter the world of others. We forge bonds of solidarity with others. We dedicate ourselves to promoting the common good. We reach out to the weak and vulnerable, to those in society who are poor and marginalized. We seek to live in fellowship with God at all times. We strive to seek God in all events and circumstances. We celebrate the sacrament of the present moment. We live in the hope of our full and final transformation in Christ.

When practicing contemplative ethics, we acknowledge and celebrate the personal ground of reality. We live in close communion with the Father and seek to share this relationship with others. We view everything that happens to us in life in the light of our relationship to the Father. We contemplate the people and events around us. We listen to others and ponder what they say. We empty ourselves in service to others. We view our lives in terms of mission. We forge bonds of communion and solidarity with others. We mission in community. We live simply and without clutter. We find time for prayer. We read the scriptures as a way of discerning the Father's will for us. We value purity of heart and seek to foster it in others. We find the words that will touch people's hearts and draw them closer to Christ. We receive the sacraments and view them as unique opportunities to encounter Christ and be touched by his grace.

When practicing contemplative ethics, we seek to do the

will of God in all things. We embrace whatever suffering comes our way when doing God's will. We look upon Jesus' dying words as a testament that he left behind to guide us in times of suffering. We forgive those who harm us. We yearn for paradise, the peace of God's kingdom. We look to Mary as our mother. We trust in God in times of desolation. We thirst for God. We bear suffering that befalls us courageously. We bring our suffering and needs to God through prayer. We listen to God's Word and, through it, seek to understand God's will for us. We act upon our discernment of God's will for us. We devote ourselves fully to the task God gives us. We look beyond our present suffering. We persevere to the end.

Finally, when practicing contemplative ethics, we embrace death as a part of life. We look beyond the present world. We believe in miracles. We seek to foster intimacy in our relationships. We trust the testimony of the apostles. We believe that love is stronger than death. We live in hope. We believe that the idea of resurrection became a reality in the person of Jesus. We believe that Jesus' resurrection marks the beginning of a new creation, and we yearn for its coming. We believe that through baptism we are incorporated into Christ's paschal mystery and become members of his Body. We live without fear. We live in peace and seek to promote it. We proclaim to all the world the Good News of life in the risen Christ. We believe that, although the Risen Lord has returned to the Father, he is still with us and will remain so forever. We believe that we receive a foretaste of the resurrection whenever we celebrate at the table of the Lord.

Contemplative ethics is all about contemplating the face of Christ and allowing ourselves to be contemplated by him. By breaking out of the self-imposed prison of the rational and psychological world that has shaped much of Catholic moral theology's past, it seeks an integration of theory and practice, spirituality and morality, contemplation and action that will root the discipline in an integral trinitarian humanism. As such, it seeks the response to the Lord's command, "Put out into the deep water" (*"Duc in altum"*),[1] and represents a challenge for Catholic moral theology as it navigates the twenty-first century and sails into the deep waters of the new millennium.

# Notes

## Introduction

1. See, for example, Tullo Goffi, *Etico spirituale: Dissonanze nell'unitaria armonia* (Bologna: Edizioni Dehoniane Bologna, 1984); Sergio Bastianel L, *La preghiera nella vita morale cristiana* (Casale Monferrato: Edizioni Piemme, 1986); Maurice Zundel, *Morale et mystique* (Quebec: Editions Anne Sigier, 1986); Michael K. Duffy, *Be Blessed in What You Do: The Unity of Christian Ethics and Spirituality* (New York/Mahwah, NJ: Paulist Press, 1988); Neil Brown, *Spirit of the World: The Moral Basis of Christian Spirituality* (Manly, New South Wales, Australia: Catholic Institute of Sydney, 1990); Mark O'Keefe, *Becoming Good, Becoming Holy: On the Relationship of Christian Ethics and Spirituality* (New York/Mahwah, NJ: Paulist Press, 1995); Dennis J. Billy and Donna L. Orsuto, eds., *Spirituality and Morality: Integrating Prayer and Action* (New York/Mahwah, NJ: Paulist Press, 1996); Marciano Vidal, *Moral y espiritualidad: De la separación a la convergencia* (Madrid: Editorial El Perpetuo Socorro, 1997); Richard M. Gula, *The Call to Holiness: Embracing a Fully Christian Life* (New York/Mahwah, NJ: Paulist Press, 2003); Gula, *The Good Life: Where Morality and Spirituality Converge* (New York/Mahwah, NJ: Paulist Press, 1999); Gula, "Morality and Spirituality," in *Moral Theology: New Directions and Fundamental Issues*, ed. James Keating (New York/Mahwah, NJ: Paulist Press, 2004), 162–77; William C. Spohn, "Spirituality and Ethics: Exploring the Connections," *Theological Studies* 58 (1997): 109–23;

Spohn, *Go and Do Likewise: Jesus and Ethics* (New York: Continuum, 1999). See also journal issues dedicated to spirituality and ethics in *The Way Supplement* 88 (1997) and *Listening* 34 (1999).

2. *Conscience and Prayer: The Spirit of Catholic Moral Theology*, with James Keating (Collegeville, MN: Liturgical Press, 2001).

3. *The Way of Mystery: The Eucharist and Moral Living*, with James Keating (New York/Mahwah, NJ: Paulist Press), 2005.

4. Luke 5:4.

5. John Paul II, *Novo millennio ineunte*, nos. 1, 58–59.

6. For more on the nature of contemplation, see Michael Downey, ed., *The New Dictionary of Catholic Spirituality* (Collegeville, MN: Liturgical Press, 1993), s.v. "Contemplation, Contemplative Prayer," by William H. Shannon; L. Borriello, E. Caruna, M. R. Del Genio, N. Suffi, eds., *Dizionario di mistica* (Città di Vaticano: Libreria Editrice Vaticana, 1998), s.v. "Contemplazione," by B. Merriman. For a presentation of the various methods of Christian meditation, see Giacomo Lercaro, *Metodi di orazione mentale*, 2d ed. (Genova/Milano: Bevilacqua & Solari/Editrice Massimo, 1957), esp. 5, 91, 120, 146, 171, 216.

7. For what is involved in fostering a contemplative attitude toward life, see William A. Barry and William J. Connolly, *The Practice of Spiritual Direction* (Minneapolis, MN: Seabury Press, 1982), 46–64.

8. The phrase *contemplative ethics* has its origins in a meeting Dennis J. Billy, Beverly J. Lanzetta, and Thomas M. Santa held at Mt. St. Alphonsus Retreat Center, Esopus, New York, in November 2002 to discuss the development of a continuing education program (offering CEUs) on the topic of contemplation and morality to be offered at the Redemptorist Renewal Center at Picture Rocks in Cortaro, Arizona. During the discussions, Billy suggested naming the program *The Institute for Contemplative Ethics*. The Institute was established

under that name at Picture Rocks in a joint effort by the Renewal Center and the Alphonsian Academy in Rome and was convened January 9–14, 2005. In the Christian tradition, "contemplative ethics" corresponds most closely to the integrative model of the relationship between spirituality and morality, especially as it was developed in monastic theology. See Dennis J. Billy, "Models and Multivalence: On the Interaction between Spirituality and Moral Theology," *Studia moralia* 38 (2000): 49–52.

9. William Johnston, *Mystical Theology: The Science of Love* (London: HarperCollins, 1995), 9.

## Chapter One

1. Jean Daniélou, *Myth and Mystery*, trans. P. J. Hepburne-Scott (New York: Hawthorn Books, 1968), 136.

2. For the etymology of the word *contemplation*, see Downey, ed., *The New Catholic Dictionary of Catholic Spirituality*, s.v., "Contemplation, Contemplative Prayer," by William H. Shannon.

3. For a discussion of these categories, see Romano Guardini, *Prayer in Practice*, trans. Leopold of Loewenstein-Wertheim (New York: Pantheon, 1971), 120–57. Guardini refers to *meditatio* as "inward prayer" and *contemplatio* as "mystic prayer."

4. Thomas Merton, *Seeds of Contemplation* (London: The Catholic Book Club, 1950), 32.

5. See Otfried Höffe, *Dictionnaire de morale*, adapted and augmented by Philibert Secretan (Fribourg, Switzerland / Paris: Éditions Universitaires / Éditions du Cerf, 1983), s.v. "Ethique," by Otfried Höffe; Battista Mondin, *Dizionario enciclopedico del pensiero di San Tommaso d'Aquino* (Bologna: Edizioni Studio Dominicano, 1991), s.v. "Etica."

6. For a treatment of conflicting ethical traditions, see Alasdair MacIntyre, *Three Rival Versions of Moral Enquiry:*

*Encyclopedia, Genealogy, and Tradition* (Notre Dame, IN: University of Notre Dame Press, 1990); MacIntyre, *Whose Justice? Which Rationality?* (Notre Dame, IN: University of Notre Dame Press, 1988), 389–403. For various definitions of Christian ethics, see Servais Pinckaers, *The Sources of Christian Ethics*, trans. Sr. Mary Thomas Noble (Washington, DC: Catholic University of America Press, 1995), 1–13.

7. Herein, Introduction, n. 1.

8. Thomas Merton, *Contemplation in a World of Action* (Garden City, NY: Image Books, 1973), 179.

9. According to Karl Rahner, "The Trinity of the economy of salvation *is* the immanent Trinity and vice versa." "Remarks on the Dogmatic Treatise 'De Trinitate,'" in *Theological Investigations*, vol. 4, *More Recent Writings*, trans. Kevin Smyth (London: Darton, Longman and Todd, 1974), 87.

10. Gen 1:27; *Catechism of the Catholic Church*, nos. 1701–9; International Theological Commission, "Communion and Stewardship: Human Persons Created in the Image of God," *Origins* 34 (no. 15, 2004): 233–48.

11. Augustine, *De Trinitate*, 14.11.

12. For an expanded presentation, see Dennis J. Billy, "Dialoguing with Human Experience: The Challenge to Catholic Moral Theology," in *Moral Theology: New Directions and Fundamental Issues*, 69–87.

13. Luke 15:11–32.

14. For the relationship between the sacred and historical dimensions of time, see Hans Urs von Balthasar, *A Theological Anthropology* (New York: Sheed and Ward, 1967), 1–42.

15. Contemplation, communion, and mission were identified by the late Pope John Paul II as three important duties for Christians in the world today. See his Angelus of Sunday, September 5, 2004.

16. For a discussion of attitudes and options, see Fabio Giardini, *Pray without Ceasing: Toward a Systematic Psycho-*

*theology of Christian Prayerlife* (Leominster, Herefordshire/ Rome: Gracewing/Millennium, 1998), 361–95.

17. Merton, *Seeds of Contemplation*, 33.

# Chapter Two

1. Balthasar, *A Theological Anthropology*, 301.

2. For Christ as the language of God, see ibid., 275–305.

3. See Joseph A. Komonchak, Mary Collins, and Dermot A. Lane, eds., *The New Dictionary of Theology* (Dublin: Gill and Macmillan, 1987), s.v. "Logos," by Anthony J. Kelly.

4. *The Roman Missal: The Sacramentary* (New York: Catholic Book Publishing Co., 1985), 368.

5. Walter Kasper, *The God of Jesus Christ*, trans. Matthew J. O'Connell (New York: Crossroad, 1984), 280.

6. This paragraph is adapted from Dennis J. Billy, *Evangelical Kernels: A Theological Spirituality of the Religious Life* (Staten Island, NY: Alba House, 1993), 36–37.

7. The classical definition of *person* is "the individual (incommunicable) substance of a rational nature." See Boethius, *De duabus naturis*, 3. Gerald O'Collins describes a person as "this rational and free individual, who is the subject and center of action and relationships and who enjoys incommunicable identity, inalienable dignity, and inviolable rights." *Christology: A Biblical, Historical, and Systematic Study of Jesus* (Oxford: Oxford University Press, 1995), 235.

8. *Catechism of the Catholic Church*, no. 468.

9. For a description of the theological significance of Rublev's *The Holy Trinity*, see M. Helen Weier, *Festal Icons of the Lord* (Collegeville, MN: Liturgical Press, 1977), 49–53.

10. Merton, *Seeds of Contemplation*, 88.

11. See, for example, Pseudo-Dionysius, *The Divine Names*, chap. 4, sect. 20.

12. Gen 1:27; *Catechism of the Catholic Church*, nos 1701–9; International Theological Commission, "Communion and Stewardship: Human Persons Created in the Image of God," *Origins* 34 (2004): 233–48.

13. Thus scholastic theologians speak of the healing and elevating function of Christ's redeeming grace (*gratia elevans et sanans*). See Ludwig Ott, *Fundamentals of Catholic Dogma*, trans. Patrick Lynch (Rockford, IL: Tan Books and Publishers, 1974), 221.

14. Athanasius, *De incarnatione*, 54.3.

15. Merton, *Seeds of Contemplation*, 89.

# Chapter Three

1. Teilhard de Chardin, *Forma Christi* (1918). Cited in Henri de Lubac, *Teilhard de Chardin: The Man and His Meaning*, trans. René Hague (New York: Mentor-Omega, 1965), 37–38.

2. Rom 6:3–5.

3. John 1:14.

4. Helmut Koester, *Introduction to the New Testament*, vol. 2, *History and Literature of Early Christianity* (Philadelphia: Fortress Press, 1982), 188–89. For Christianity's life-and-death struggle with docetic Gnosticism, see Walter Kasper, *Jesus the Christ*, trans. V. Green (London: Burns and Oates, 1976), 197–207.

5. Again, Athanasius, *De incarnatione*, 54.3.

6. For the development of the Church's christological teachings from Nicaea to Chalcedon, see J. N. D. Kelly, *Early Christian Doctrines* (New York: Harper & Row, 1978; revised ed.), 223–51, 280–343. For corresponding documentation, see J. Neuner and J. Dupuis, eds., *The Christian Faith in the Doctrinal Documents of the Catholic Church*, 7th ed. (New York: Alba House, 2001), 218–28.

7. For a summary of the Church's teaching on the Incarnate Word, see *Catechism of the Catholic Church*, nos. 456–83. For the relationship between the divine and human in Christ, see O'Collins, *Christology*, 224–49.

8. In the words of Kasper: "The Church cannot regard itself...as a closed system. It must enter on a spiritual exchange and an intellectual discussion with the world. In this, it must on the one hand pay heed to the external prophecy of the world, yet on the other bear witness that in Jesus Christ alone the hopes of mankind have been fulfilled in a unique and unsurpassable way; and that he is the great Amen to all promises," *Jesus the Christ*, 268.

9. Matt 1–2; Luke 1–2.

10. Matt 18:2; Mark 10:15; Luke 18:17.

11. Matt 1:23.

12. Balthasar, *A Theological Anthropology*, 254.

13. O'Collins, *Christology*, 248.

14. Thomas Merton, *No Man Is an Island* (Garden City, NY: Doubleday, 1955), 187.

15. John 14:6.

16. This phrase is part of the mystical vocabulary of Nicholas of Cusa and is applied here analogously to the relationship between the divine and human natures of Christ. See F. C. Happold, *Mysticism: A Study and an Anthology* (New York: Penguin Books, 1970; reprint, 1984), 333–41.

17. For a treatment of contemplation and liturgy, see Cyprian Vagaggini, *Theological Dimensions of the Liturgy: A General Treatise on the Theology of the Liturgy*, 4th ed., trans. Leonard J. Doyle and W. A. Jurgens (Collegeville, MN: Liturgical Press, 1976), 734–36.

18. Matt 1:23.

19. Merton, *No Man Is an Island*, 101.

20. Matt 19:14.

21. 1 Cor 15:22; Col 3:9–10.

22. For a treatment of the personal, societal, and universal levels of sin, see Billy, *Evangelical Kernels*, 65–76.

23. Mark 14:36.

24. For more on the sacrament of the present moment, see Jean-Pierre de Caussade, *Abandonment to Divine Providence*, trans. John Beevers (Garden City, NY: Image, 1975), 36–58; and de Caussade, *The Sacrament of the Present Moment*, trans. Kitty Muggeridge (San Francisco: Harper, 1982).

25. See above, this chapter, n. 16.

# Chapter Four

1. Walter Kasper, *Jesus the Christ*, 70.

2. For a summary of the mysteries of Jesus' hidden and public lives, see *Catechism of the Catholic Church*, nos. 512–70. For a more extended treatment, see Jacques Duquesne, *Jesus: An Unconventional Biography* (Liguori, MO: Triumph Books, 1997).

3. For a bibliographical survey of the quest for the historical Jesus, see Raymond E. Brown, *An Introduction to the New Testament* (New York: Doubleday, 1997), 817–30. For changing perceptions of Jesus through history, see Jaroslav Pelikan, *Jesus through the Centuries* (New Haven, CT/London: Yale University Press, 1985).

4. For the main characteristics of Catholic scriptural interpretation, see the Pontifical Biblical Commission, *The Interpretation of the Bible in the Church* (Vatican City: Libreria Editrice Vaticana, 1993), 86–127.

5. The First Council of Nicaea, *Expositio fidei CCCXVIII patrum*, in *Decrees of the Ecumenical Councils*, English ed., Norman P. Tanner, vol. 1 (London/Washington, DC: Sheed and Ward/Georgetown University Press, 1990), 5. See also *Catechism of the Catholic Church*, nos. 430–55. For the sources of revelation and its authentic interpretation, see *Dei verbum*, no. 10, in

*Decrees of the Ecumenical Councils,* vol. 2, 975. See also *Catechism of the Catholic Church,* nos. 74–95. For the characteristics of the Catholic interpretation of scripture, see the Pontifical Biblical Commission, *The Interpretation of the Bible in the Church,* 86–112.

6. Second Vatican Council, *Dei verbum,* nos. 17–20, in *Decrees of the Ecumenical Councils,* vol. 2, 978–79. For a treatment of Christ as the norm of history, see Hans Urs von Balthasar, *A Theology of History* (New York: Sheed and Ward, 1963), 79–107.

7. For the universal dimensions of Christ's redemptive action, see Collins, *Christology,* 296–305.

8. John 15:15.

9. Rom 8:14–17.

10. Luke 15:11–31.

11. Second Vatican Council, *Lumen gentium,* nos. 2–4, in *Decrees of the Ecumenical Councils,* vol. 2, 850–51. See also *Catechism of the Catholic Church,* nos. 514–570.

12. For more on the nature of these kingdom-oriented relationships, see Hans Urs von Balthasar, *The God Question & Modern Man,* trans. Hilda Graef (New York: Seabury Press, 1967), 142–55.

13. For how Jesus' status as Son and Word of God permeates every facet of his life, see Hans Urs von Balthasar, *A Theological Anthropology* (New York: Sheed and Ward, 1967), 246–47.

14. Thomas Merton, *Life and Holiness* (Garden City, NY: Image Books, 1964), 26.

15. John 19:25–27.

16. For a consideration of Jesus' conscious knowledge, see Raymond E. Brown, *Jesus, God and Man* (New York/London: Macmillan/Collier Macmillan, 1967), 39–102. For a treatment of Jesus' understanding of his Divine Sonship, see O'Collins, *Christology,* 113–35. See also Kasper, *The God of Jesus Christ,* 158–97.

17. For a consideration of Jesus' earthly ministry, see Kasper, *Jesus the Christ*, 63–123; and Kasper, *The God of Jesus Christ*, 166–72.

18. Matt 6:10.

19. For a consideration of Jesus' sanctifying and redemptive role in human history, see Hans Urs von Balthasar, *A Theology of History*, 49–75.

20. Matt 3:13–17; Mark 1:9–11; Luke 3:31–22.

21. Matt 26:26–29; Mark 14:22–25; Luke 22:15–20.

22. Gal 2:20.

23. Thomas Merton, *No Man Is an Island*, 143.

24 Matt 16:15–16.

25. Gen 1:26–27.

26. Matt 10: 1–4; Mark 3:13–19; Luke 6:12–16.

27. Luke 10:1–16.

28. Matt 8:20; Luke 9:58.

29. Matt 4:1–11; Mark 1:12–13; Luke 1–13.

30. Matt 14:23; Mark 6:46; Luke 6:12, 9:28.

31. Mark 1:27; Luke 4:32, 36.

32. Matt 5:8.

33. Luke 9:62.

34. For more on Christ's mystical life in his members, see Jean-Pierre de Caussade, *Abandonment to Divine Providence*, trans. John Beevers, 44–46.

35. Mark 1:17.

# Chapter Five

1. Thomas Merton, *No Man Is an Island*, 77–78.

2. Horace Bushnell, *The Vicarious Sacrifice* (1866), 35–36. Cited in Kenneth Leech, *Experiencing God: Theology as Spirituality* (San Francisco: Harper & Row, 1985), 301.

3. 1 John 4:8.

4. Matt 27:46; Luke 23:34, 43, 46; John 19:26–27, 28, 30. For a treatment of Jesus' "Seven Last Words," see Berard L. Marthaler, gen. ed., *The New Catholic Encyclopedia*, 2d cd. (Detroit: Thomson/Gale, 2003), s.v. "Seven Last Words," by S. Makarewicz.

5. Luke 23:34.

6. Luke 23:43.

7. See Alphonsus de Liguori, *The Way to Converse Always and Familiarly with God*, in *The Complete Works of Saint Alphonsus de Liguori*, vol. 2 (Brooklyn: Redemptorist Fathers, 1926), 395.

8. John 19:26–27.

9. Matt. 27:46.

10. John 19:28.

11. John 19:30.

12. Luke 23:46.

13. John 19:34.

14. John 10:30.

15. John 1:14.

16. The word *sacrifice* comes from the Latin *sacrificium*, which is itself a composite of the words *sacer* ("holy") and *facere* ("to make").

17. Athanasius of Alexandria, *De incarnatione*, 54.3 [SC 199:458–59; PG 25:191–92]; Gregory of Nyssa, *De opificio hominis*, 16 [SC 6:151–61; PG 44:178–88].

18. Matt 16:21–23, 17:22–23, 20:17–19; Mark 8:31–33, 9:30–32, 10:32–34; Luke 9:22, 9:43–45, 18:28–30.

19. Matt 14:22–33; Mark 6:45–52; John 6:16–21. See also John L. McKenzie, "The Gospel According to Matthew," in *The Jerome Biblical Commentary*, ed. Raymond E. Brown, Joseph A. Fitzmeyer, and Roland E. Murphy (Englewood Cliffs, NJ: Prentice-Hall, 1968), 89.

20. Weier, *Festal Icons of the Lord*, 19–22.

21. Matt 21:1–11; Mark 11:1–11; Luke 19:28–38; John 12:12–16.
22. Matt. 21:12–17; Mark 11:15–19; Luke 19:45–48; John 2:14–16.
23. Matt 26:14–16; Mark 14: 10–11; Luke 22:3–6.
24. Matt 26:69–75; Mark 14:66–72; Luke 22:55–62; John 18:15–18, 25–27.
25. Matt 27:55–56; Mark 15:40–41; Luke 23:49; John 19:25–27.
26. Matt 27; Mark 15; Luke 23; John 18–19.
27. Matt 26–27; Mark 14–15; Luke 22–23; John 18–19.
28. Matt 26:30–46; Mark 14:32–42; Luke 22:40–46; John 18:1–11.
29. Luke 22:42–44.
30. Matt 27:46.
31. Luke 23:46.
32. Matt 26–27; Mark 14–15; Luke 22–23; John 18–19.
33. Merton, No Man Is an Island, 134.
34. Matt 6:10.
35. Luke 23:34.
36. See William A. Meninger, The Process of Forgiveness (New York: Continuum, 1997), 48–72.
37. Luke 23:43.
38. John 19:26–27.
39. Matt 27:46.
40. John 19:28.
41. John 19:30.
42. Luke 23:46.
43. John 15:16.
44. Rom 8:15.
45. Bushnell, cited in Leech, 301.

# Chapter Six

1. Francis Xavier Durrwell, *Christ Our Passover: The Indispensable Role of Resurrection in Our Salvation*, trans. John F. Craghan (Liguori, MO: Liguori Publications, 2004), 172.
2. Ibid., 1.
3. Rev 22:13.
4. Acts 9:1–19.
5. 2 Cor 5:7.
6. Matt 19:26; Mark 10:27; Luke 1:37, 18:27.
7. For late Jewish ideas about the afterlife and the distinctiveness of the early Christian proclamation, see Edward Schillebeeckx, *Jesus: An Experiment in Christology*, trans. Hubert Hoskins (New York: Crossroad, 1985), 518–25.
8. According to Raymond E. Brown, "While the risen Jesus stood outside the bounds of space and time, by his appearance he touched the lives of men who were in space and time, men who were in history. The interaction between the eschatological and the historical should not be lost sight of." *The Virginal Conception and the Bodily Resurrection of Jesus* (New York: Paulist Press, 1973), 126.
9. On "apostolicity" as an identifying mark of the Church, see John Macquarrie, *Principles of Christian Theology* (Grand Rapids, MI: Eerdmans, 1991), 126.
10. Despite this vast, encompassing vision of the redemptive value of the Easter event, the possibility that some people will exercise their human freedom in such a way so as to refuse God's gift of salvation will always remain, unless, of course, one embraces the rather tenuous doctrine of Origen's *apokatasis* (i.e., the ultimate restoration to God of all created beings—even devils). This section of the chapter draws upon my treatment of the resurrection in Billy, *Evangelical Kernels*, 111–13.
11. Merton, *Life and Holiness*, 64.
12. 1 John 4:8.

13. See, for example, Pseudo-Dionysius the Areopagite, *De divinis nominibus* 4.1, 4.4 [PG 3:693B, 697C].

14. See Kasper, *The God of Jesus Christ*, 280; Athanasius, *De synodis* [PG 26:707–12]; Gregory Nazianzus, *Oratio* 29.16 [SC 250:210–13]; Augustine, *De trinitate* 5.5 [CCL 50:210–11; PL 42:913–14]; Denz.-Schön., nos. 528–32 [278–81].

15. John 20:27.

16. This section draws upon my treatment of the Trinity in Billy, *Evangelical Kernels*, 33–48.

17. For more on the revelatory nature of the resurrection, see Gerald O'Collins, *Christology*, 97–104.

18. For the redemptive features of the resurrection, see ibid., 104–6.

19. For the resurrection as a function of divine activity, see ibid., 106–12.

20. Rom 5:12–21; Col 1:15–20. For the content of faith in Jesus' resurrection, see Walter Kasper, *Jesus the Christ*, 144–60; Durrwell, *Christ, Our Passover*, 21–59.

21. For the basis of belief in Jesus' resurrection, see Kasper, *Jesus the Christ*, 124–43; Durrwell, *Christ, Our Passover*, 1–19.

22. Luke 24:34.

23. For more on Jesus' resurrection appearances, see Raymond E. Brown, *The Virginal Conception and the Bodily Resurrection of Jesus* (New York: Paulist Press, 1973), 69–129; Dermot A. Lane, *The Reality of Jesus* (New York: Paulist Press, 1975), 44–65; John L. McKenzie, *The New Testament without Illusion* (Chicago: Thomas More Press, 1980), 197–208.

24. For more on Jesus' resurrection, his message, and the birth of the Church, see Durrwell, *Jesus Our Passover*, 61–85; O'Collins, *Christology*, 82–112.

25. Durrwell, *Christ Our Passover*, 2.

26. See Pat Collins, *Intimacy and the Hungers of the Heart* (Dublin/Mystic, CT: Columba Press/Twenty-Third Publications, 1991), 104–43.

27. Ibid., 210.
28. 1 John 4:18.
29. Clement of Alexandria, *Stromata* 7:7 [PG 9.455]; Evagrius Ponticus, *De oratione*, 3 [PG 79.1167]. Cited in Simon Tugwell, *Prayer*, vol. 1 (Dublin: Veritas Publications, 1974), vii.
30. Luke 24:30.
31. John 12:24.

# Epilogue

1. Luke 5:4.